TH

MIDDLEMAN METHOD

HOW TO BUILD A 7-FIGURE GOVCON SERVICES AGENCY THAT SUBCONTRACTS WORK AND KEEPS THE PROFITS

DEREK JAMES

The Legal Middleman Method

ISBN: 979-8-9890682-6-5

Book Design by Transcendent Publishing

Disclaimer: Derek James is not an attorney and is not credentialed to formally give legal advice. In this book, Derek shares his own viewpoints and personal experience in the small govcon industry. All regulations mentioned are cited for you to further research on your own. If you are seeking legal advice, Derek encourages you to seek proper legal counsel.

Printed in the United States of America.

"Our deepest fear is not that we are inadequate. Our deepest fear is that we are powerful beyond measure. It is our light, not our darkness that most frightens us. We ask ourselves, 'Who am I to be brilliant, gorgeous, talented, fabulous?' Actually, who are you not to be? You are a child of God. Your playing small does not serve the world. There is nothing enlightened about shrinking so that other people won't feel insecure around you. We are all meant to shine, as children do. We were born to make manifest the glory of God that is within us. It's not just in some of us; it's in everyone. And as we let our own light shine, we unconsciously give other people permission to do the same. As we are liberated from our own fear, our presence automatically liberates others."

— *Marianne Williamson*

TABLE OF CONTENTS

Introduction vii

Part I: My Story 1

Broke 3

"I Found The Salt!" 9

It's A Numbers Game 15

Look, Mom, I Did It! 19

Million Dollar List 25

Part II: The Legal Middleman Method 31

Section 1: Regulations 33

Middleman Regulations 35

Section 2: Offer 45

Agency 47

Deal or No Deal?. 55

Industries 63

Proof of Concept. 73

Umbrella Strategy 79

Section 3: Subcontractors 83
Markups. 85
Rule of 2. 91
Subcontractor Site Visit Checklist. 95
Sub Script. 101
Section 4: Bidding 109
Reading Solicitations 111
Outline 129
Pricing. 137
Proposal Writing 147
Review, Submit, Debrief 155
Section 5: Award 161
Award, What's Next? 163
Contract Management. 169
Contract Earnings Multipliers 177
Final Thoughts 187
Expectations. 193
Acknowledgments 199
About the Author. 201
Appendix 203

INTRODUCTION

Nice to meet you! I'm so happy you picked up a copy of The Legal Middleman Method. If you aren't familiar with me and my work, my name is Derek James, and I've been working in federal contracting for the past decade. I got my start in 2013 working for a small government contractor having zero experience in the industry, and in a few short years, I went on to win 32 contracts worth over $15 million dollars by my 30th birthday! Many of the contracts were able to be performed using the Legal Middleman Method, and that's exactly what you will be learning in this book.

In 2018, I left my job, and branched out to start working as a consultant to help small businesses win their first government contracts. I didn't know what I was going to find, but I was appalled by what was being taught in the space. So many things that were just so unnecessary (and expensive) were being pushed onto brand new government contractors. (Remember, I did all this with zero experience *and* in a few short years. I didn't use all these fancy shiny objects, so why do you have to?)

I also saw that there were "coaches" and consultants on YouTube and other social media platforms, telling small business owners to do something that is downright illegal. They were telling small businesses that they could win a contract and have another company fulfill all the work without regard for regulations. Period. End of story.

I almost fell out of my seat. Without more context, that is called an "illegal pass-through scheme." What happened to Limitations on Subcontracting? Simplified Acquisition Procedures/Threshold? Or, what about self-performance limits for socio-economic programs? There was nothing. (Don't know what these terms are or why they're so important? This book will have you understanding them like a pro.)

So, I've watched in disbelief as this reckless advice was being spewed for years while I stayed in "my lane" teaching SAM.gov contracting. But now I've had enough. I've written this book to set the record straight and give small business owners a real method to Legally Middleman government contracts that won't put them in harm's way.

In the Legal Middleman Method, I share my personal story of getting into government contracting so that you understand where I came from and why I have so much to share. After my story, we spend the remainder of the book breaking down exactly how to Legally Middleman government contracts. Not only will you gain understanding and the proper context to do this, but I also give you tools and resources that you can start using today to put your small business on the proper Legal Middleman path.

In this book, we are going to cover the Regulations governing the industry, so that you will be an expert at knowing the legal and illegal approaches to Middlemanning. We are going to get you clear on your Offer so you can start finding bids that are a match for your small business. I will show you how to identify

Subcontractors with scripts for reaching out to them to form teaming partnerships so that they can support you in completing the work.

You are going to learn my 5-Step Bidding Process (because you also need to learn how to put together competitive and compliant bid responses to solicitations on SAM.gov.) In it, you will learn how to read solicitations, build outlines, price, write proposals, and how to submit your offer. And lastly, you will learn what to do when you actually win a contract, including contract management, when to invoice, and a lot more to start profiting and growing a GovCon Agency.

Lastly, before we dive in and get started with my story, I must share what this book is and what this book is not. This book is not a get-rich-quick solution. When I show you how to play the Number's Game, for example, you will see how I break down your personal efforts into realistic timelines. This book is also not about "cheating the system." As I've already explained, it's quite the opposite. This book was created to counterbalance those who are spewing reckless or incomplete advice in the industry.

With that being said, so much of the Legal Middleman Method is part of my personal story. So, I know what's possible for you if you use this method. If you're looking to diversify your existing business or start a new one based solely on government contracting, this is something that you can start today.

You don't have to be a subcontractor for 2 years before attempting to bid on a government contract. You can, instead, work with subcontractors to team up on contracts and start building a GovCon Services Agency that will enable you to be your own boss, strive for financial independence, create job opportunities for your family, or even give you something to transition into if you are transitioning out of the military or from some other employment.

I have so much to share, so if you're ready, let's get started with my story.

PART I

MY STORY

BROKE

In 2013, I was 26 years old, still living at my parents' house, and I was driving a rusted, red, Pontiac Sunfire. I had over $60,000 in debt from my MBA degree, and I had just closed the doors on my failed restaurant business. I'd been hospitalized for panic attacks, and I was just old enough to get kicked off my parent's health insurance before being hospitalized. In the 3 years prior, I had 6 jobs, and the longest of which lasted 15 months. Needless to say, I was totally broke and at the end of my rope.

Amongst the dozens of jobs I had responded to was a job ad advertised through my university's career portal for a proposal writer. I remember reading the job description, and it read something like, "Business Development Proposal Writer Wanted. Build your book of business with the Army, Navy, and other government agencies." I had been a proposal writer for the 15-month grant writing assistantship that I held while in graduate school. I had no idea what a Business Development Proposal Writer was, or what the Army and Navy had to do with it. I thought it sounded exciting, and after everything I had been through recently, all I wanted was a 9-5 job with good health insurance.

I quickly got a call back after applying (from a man we will call Frank), and within a couple of weeks of interviewing and background checks, I got the job. Once I started working, it became very apparent that there wasn't a traditional training or onboarding process. I had absolutely no idea what my job was. My first day consisted of accompanying my boss to an annual NDIA (National Defense Industrial Association) Conference, that started that same week.

My boss was a very strong and persuasive lady who spoke the government contract language at ease, and I was totally intimidated by her. I was honestly intimidated by the entire event. There were guest speakers talking about tanks and war and spending budgets, and I had not the slightest clue where I fit into all of it.

During the event, my boss left early and told me to stay back and take notes on things that I thought were "important." I could hear the conversations of people around me, and I remember thinking it literally sounded like a foreign language. I had no idea what people were saying, and I had no idea what was "important." I had already begun questioning what I had gotten myself into.

The next couple of weeks were much less exciting. I still had no training, and the only thing I was told to do was to go to a website called FBO.gov and look for "opportunities" for our company to bid on. FBO.gov (Federal Business Opportunities) is the commonly used website for seeking federal government contracts. FBO.gov is free and has everything you need to win contracts.

When the government has work that needs to be done, they post the requirement on FBO, and then small businesses bid for the work and win the contract. (Please note that FBO is the new SAM.gov. The websites have transitioned since my story. As I reference FBO, think SAM.gov)

I had a lot of immediate challenges with this. First, I had no idea how to use this website. Second, I didn't know what an "opportunity" was or what that meant. More importantly, I didn't even know what my company did. It ended up taking me a year to understand what government contracting was, and to be able to explain it to my friends and family.

Until that point, I would just say, "I can't really put what I do into words, but it's with the government." It sounded impressive enough. I remained extremely overwhelmed, and I was drinking from a fire hose daily. Without any real training, I was struggling to make sense of this completely alien job that I had wandered into.

My boss was a very busy lady, but after a few weeks of being there, she assigned me to my first proposal. Ah-ha, I was saved! A proposal to work on. This was something I could mentally conceive of, and since I was hired to be a proposal writer, it made perfect sense that I would work on a proposal, right? This may sound overly facetious, but at the time, that's exactly how I felt.

The proposal was for a GSA contract called OASIS (One Acquisition Solution for Integrated Services). OASIS is a rather large government contract vehicle that allows only pre-vetted winners to bid on the task orders. It serves as a MATOC (Multiple Award Task Order Contract), where there are multiple winners that become part of a pool, and then only the winners are qualified to bid on task orders (jobs) as they are released.

Looking back, assigning me to the OASIS proposal with zero experience was setting me up for failure. Everything was still alphabet soup to me, so it made reading the proposal requirements painfully slow. I had experience in grant writing in the non-profit world, but very little carried over to writing government proposals. My boss brought in an experienced proposal writer, and even she seemed to be having a hard time with it, so I didn't feel so bad.

There were a lot of questions being submitted to the government from other companies as well. The proposal submission requirements were very contradictory and confusing to everyone. (I'm telling you this in case you are going through the same experience!) Our company didn't have great past performance either, so it became a struggle to put together the right mix of experience required for a winning proposal, and in the end, we lost. We'll come back to this shortly, and you'll see how I became the fall guy for this ...

During my entire first year, Frank was the only one who took me under his wing. I didn't really talk to anyone else in the office. Frank was a retired Army Vet, and he seemed to take a liking to me. He was a recruiter by trade but served as "the executioner" whenever my boss needed him to be the bad guy. He had a huge heart and helped anyone who needed it. I'm forever grateful to him. He hired me, and during my first year, he literally became the reason I continued working there ... although I wouldn't be writing proposals as I had originally thought.

One day, after about 2 months on the job, I saw Frank get called into my boss's office. He shut the see-through glass door and locked it, and I watched my boss and Frank start yelling at each other. To my surprise, they were arguing and pointing in the direction of my cubicle. It didn't take long to realize what (or who) they were arguing about. It was me!

My boss wanted to fire me because of what happened with the OASIS proposal. Frank was in there fighting for me to convince her to give me another chance. When Frank came out, he motioned for me to come walk with him, and we carried on in silence to his office at the other side of the building.

He sat me down and said, "Proposals aren't your cup of tea, are they?" I replied, "I don't mind writing proposals, I'm just very new, and I don't understand a lot." "I know", he said, empathizing with my situation. "Well, she wants to fire you, but I told her you have a lot of potential. How do you feel about doing business development instead?" I replied, "What is that?" "Well, it's more based on people, developing relationships, and marketing the company." I said, "I need a job, and I'm willing to learn, so I can do that." He said, "Okay, next Monday you will start doing BD."

"I FOUND THE SALT!"

My company had certain socioeconomic advantages that allowed us to go after contracts that were "set-aside." Examples of set-asides include Small Disadvantaged Business, Economically Disadvantaged Woman-Owned Small Businesses, Service-Disabled Veteran Owned Small Business (SDVOSB), Hub Zone, 8(a), and Native American Businesses.

The need for set-asides is because smaller businesses are not as equipped as large businesses to compete for government contracts. In response to this disparity, government agencies will "set-aside" certain contracts during procurement to help level the playing field.

My company had set-asides for Woman-Owned Small Business, and we were also an 8(a). The 8(a) is a designation that lasts for 9 years, and it is appointed by the SBA (Small Business Administration). In a nutshell, during the nine-year 8(a) status, the SBA becomes a type of incubator for the small business to grow and win contracts. Through this arrangement, the small business is able to win contracts that are called "sole-source" or "direct award contracts," where there is no competition required. Wait, what? Yes, that's correct, an 8(a) company can win contracts with no competition.

STOP. If you are not an 8(a) company and you do not qualify to be an 8(a) company, you are probably about to check out of this book. Do not do that. You don't need special set-asides to follow my method, they will only act as a bonus if you have them. I speak of sole-sourcing in my story because it was part of my journey. Only around half of my total contracts won were sole sourced, and the other half were small business competed contracts. The remaining sections of the book focus on competed contracts. So, if you don't have socio-economic set-asides, there is plenty of opportunity for you with small business set-aside contracts, and I will discuss much more about this later in this book.

Back to the story.

Monday had arrived, and I was to officially begin doing business development. Frank had explained the 8(a) sole-source opportunity to me, and he said this was the easiest way for me to begin winning contracts. My boss also spent some time with me during the week to further explain how I could win contracts. I was grateful to get any sliver of time with her that she'd give me. She told me that all I had to do was start responding to the government's request for market research and let them know we're an 8(a) and we're able to do a sole source.

This seemed overly simple to me, but it was something I could wrap my head around, and I knew it would keep me busy. She also said it would be good for me to call the Contracting Officers and Contract Specialists who were listed as the point of contact for the market research. I had no idea what to say to them, but this is exactly what I started doing.

I spent most of my days on FBO looking at different sources sought (market research notices). I felt very lost most of the time. I still didn't really know what our company did or sold. I felt almost depressed because I wanted to win, but I felt I was going nowhere fast. It's disenchanting when you keep putting in work, and there are no tangible results to show for it. Even worse, I wasn't getting feedback to know whether what I was doing was right or not. I didn't want to keep working there, but I continued because I was committed to making it work, somehow.

Our company motto was "Your Needs, Our Mission," and we went after almost every kind of work. Since that was the case, I responded to a lot of market research that you wouldn't even believe. There's nothing technically wrong with going after anything and everything, but from a business standpoint and a strategic marketing standpoint, it makes you look diluted as a company.

My method will have you focusing and representing your company in the strongest light with an offer of a very focused set of solutions. Take it from me ... don't be a company that goes after everything.

Winter had come and so did my first big break. I started with the company in August, so I had started during the very busy and turbulent time of the year for government contracting. I had survived the OASIS debacle and had graduated to responding to market research on FBO, however, I still had no sole source to show for it. That was about to change.

It was December 2013, and we had received a call from a local military base. It was an exceptionally cold winter that year, and they needed road salt. All the barges had frozen to transport salt, and the local military bases were literally calling all the 8(a) companies in the area to see if they could do a sole source contract for it.

My boss was on the phone with a contracting officer, and I heard her concluding the conversation with, "No thanks, we can't provide that." When I heard this, I felt my excitement grow because I knew this was an opportunity. I walked up to my boss and propositioned her that, if I could find the salt, would she accept the contract?"

She wasn't impressed with my question, but she laughed and said, "If you think you can find it, then go right ahead." I was on a mission to find road salt, and more seriously, I wanted to prove to my boss that I could do it, and I also wanted to win my first contract!

I immediately started calling every landscape company that does year-round seasonal maintenance. They all said the same thing, "Sorry, we can't keep up with the customers we already have." It was an awfully cold winter. I worked on this for two weeks. I was calling everywhere I could think of to no avail.

I started getting creative, and at one point, I started calling the out-of-state salt mines. I thought if I could secure the salt, then all I had to do was contact a trucking company for the pickup and delivery. However, the problem with this strategy was that the freight costs were going to be so high, and I knew there was no way the government would agree to our price.

I kept calling until I finally found a landscaping company from a bordering state. They had some extra salt that met the specs of the customer (anti-caking agents), but they needed an answer quickly, otherwise, they were going to obligate the salt to someone else.

My boss had seen how hard I had been working, and I knew I gained some favor with her then. I ran up to her and said, "I found the salt." She laughed and said, "Really?" I confirmed, and she told me to call the contracting officer and ask if she was still looking for an 8(a) company to sole source this to.

I stood frozen. I had been calling on contracting officers, but I still was awful at knowing what to say. She gave me the number, and I dialed it. With a shaky voice, I introduced myself and reminded the contracting officer that she had called two weeks prior asking about the road salt.

She replied, "Yes, I remember. Are you able to provide salt per the specs in the PWS?" I didn't know what a PWS was, but I answered "yes" anyway. She asked me if my boss was around, so I put my boss on the phone with her, and she smiled as she validated my claims to the contracting officer on our ability to perform.

After that, we locked in the landscape company as our subcontractor to provide the salt in accordance with the specifications in the PWS (Performance of Work Statement or Statement of Work). Contracting and the SBA accepted the contract as a sole source, and we were awarded $89,000 to perform on the contract.

I had to go out of town the week the delivery was scheduled, so Frank ended up being our project manager onsite at the delivery. The customer was ecstatic to have the salt, and I was overjoyed to prove myself. That winter I was called the *Salt King* by my boss and everyone I worked with.

At that time, my beliefs about my ability to win a contract had begun to change. I had won one, so what was stopping me from winning more? Things really started feeling exciting for me.

IT'S A NUMBERS GAME

Spring had arrived, and I had spent the months following my big win responding to market research and advertising our 8(a). I knew it was the slow time of year for the government. The fiscal calendar for the government runs from October 1 to September 30, and their budgets are largely funded in the second half of the calendar. Most agencies get their funding in the 3rd and 4th quarters, which makes for a very slow winter and then a very busy spring and summer.

With all the responses I had submitted to market research throughout the winter, I had heard crickets back in return. I was okay with that, though, because I was practicing being very disciplined. I wanted to respond to at least 2 sources sought (aka market research) per day. I thought if I could respond to 2 per day, that would be 10 per week, and then 40 per month! Having sold insurance in one of my previous jobs, the one thing I learned was that sales is a numbers game, and I put that methodology to work.

As winter was thawing, so was my luck. The phone rang, and I answered a call from a contracting officer with the Air Force. To my surprise, he asked for me by name and continued stating that I had responded to his market research in the winter for video teleconferencing (VTC) equipment installation and maintenance. He asked if we were still interested in the work, and that he wanted to use our 8(a) for a direct award.

I remember my jaw dropping, not sure what to say, because I was about to potentially win my second contract. I quickly responded that we were still interested. He confirmed and said he would send me an email with the PWS so that we could start reviewing the work.

I hung up the phone and ran to my boss to tell her the good news. She was calm and collected (not easily excited), but still delighted by the news. I wanted to do a cartwheel. We put together our pricing proposal (which is still part of the requirement of the 8(a) sole-source), and then submitted it. With only a little negotiation, we locked in the contract for approximately $450,000!

I felt like I was on top of the world. I thought I had figured it all out. All I had to do was play the numbers game by responding to market research, and I would win. That was good enough for me at the time. And considering that no one else in the office was selling anything, I started to climb to the top. Now, others started coming to me with their questions.

At this time, I started making my own capability statements and other marketing materials. I also brought in one of my friends to make a more legitimate website that would better market our company. He also revised our logo, business cards, and branding for our marketing materials.

I started to learn how to write our past performances and match them to the requirements that were advertised in the market research. I was learning so much, and the results were very validating for me. Having been thrown into the deep end and almost fired was finally paying off.

My first year's annual performance review came 4 months late, but my boss wanted me to know that she started to see my value. I was still driving the red, stick shift, 1999 Pontiac Sunfire. The gas cap had rusted off. The passenger side had gotten hit in an accident, and my trunk would no longer open.

I don't know if she was just embarrassed to have me drive to customers with that vehicle (I'm sure she was), or if she wanted to give me encouragement. But she went with me to a Honda dealer and told me to pick out a color of the Honda Civics. I did, and then she said, "Okay it's yours."

I couldn't believe it! I felt like I hit the lottery at that moment. It may have been small peanuts to her, but I went home that night and cried. I was still in so much debt, and I didn't know how much longer my car would last. I felt so blessed.

LOOK, MOM, I DID IT!

So far that year, I'd won multiple contracts that were the same size or larger than the Air Force contract. I thought it couldn't get any better, but then it did.

We had a second bona fide office set up in a neighboring state, and a call had come in for that location to inquire if our 8(a) status was still active. I replied that we were rather new to the program, and we still had 7 of the 9 years remaining. The contracting officer said she wanted to set up a site visit for us to come out and look at the work.

I was incredibly nervous, but I was at least traveling with our construction manager. At the site, we met with the contracting officer (KO), the contracting specialist, as well as the government's engineer, who would be the appointed COR (Contracting Officer Representative) on the contract. The construction manager and I walked through the grounds, reviewed the PWS, and took photos of the site.

They wanted us to demo an existing firing range and build a new one. I couldn't believe what crazy work I'd gotten myself into. Remember when I said I thought it couldn't get any better? Well, when we finished walking the grounds, the contracting officer asked, "While you're here, do you want to look at some other work?" My construction manager and I looked at each other in excitement, and then nodded "Yes." She showed us 4 additional jobs, and we ended up winning all 5 contracts sole sourced, for a total value of over 1 million dollars!

My boss and colleagues had started to see that I was really becoming successful at winning sole-source contracts. In an office of about 25 people, no one else was selling anything besides my boss and myself. There were 3 interns (ages 19-22) that my boss would ask to do random things for proposals and watch searches we had set up on FBO.

Since they were already familiar with a little bit of the language and how to use FBO, my boss decided she wanted me to try teaching them the method I had used for sole sourcing. It was a huge compliment to be given the task, and I was up for the challenge.

I immediately went to work creating a PowerPoint presentation to train the interns. They didn't seem as excited about learning as I was to teach, but they heard me out. All I wanted them to grasp was finding decent sources sought that we could respond to. Once they found one, I would point them to a variety of capability statements I'd already created and just have them customize it to fit the specific needs addressed in the market research. They grasped it and quickly got to work.

When I took on the training, I had basically displaced myself out of a job of responding to sources sought, so I had to figure out what else I could do to win contracts. I had looked at RFPs and Solicitations on FBO before, but after the OASIS incident, I hadn't tried writing any more proposals. We didn't really have a bid/no bid system in place at the company, it was everyone for him- or herself, so I started looking at solicitations on FBO.

I knew there was a lot more opportunity if you could write winning proposals. But it was also a lot more work to do and knowledge that I didn't have. I started looking at RFPs that were easier for me to respond to, and I started putting together what I knew in a proposal. I found a quality control plan, I used the past performances from our capability statements, and then I sat with our estimator to do pricing for the proposals.

I'd submitted three proposals over the course of about 2 months and had heard nothing back. I tried following up with the contracting specialist, but they wouldn't return my phone calls or emails.

It can be hard to get hold of contracting during this time. During the solicitation stage, everything is supposed to be in writing to a contracting official because they have to be careful not to give information to one contractor that would benefit another. This would create unfair competition and is a big no-no in this game. For this reason, some contracting officials do not talk to contractors until after the award is made.

After a month went by, I heard back that we didn't win our first proposal. I was a little bummed. My boss told me to schedule something called a debrief, which is a phone call with the contracting officer where you walk through your proposal and ask questions to find out where you can improve your proposal for next time. You must request this right away. Otherwise, contracting is no longer obligated to provide the debrief. You should email a formal request for the debrief to contracting no later than 3 days after the award posting on FBO.

Looking back, we should have been a lot more consistent with requesting debriefs on losing proposals. It's so important that I incorporated it as part of the method that I'm teaching you in the second half of this book.

Shortly after the first loss, I learned that we didn't win our second proposal, either. I was okay with that because there was some excitement happening with the interns. One of the interns (Sarah) received an email back to one of her source sought responses. It was to staff one full-time employee on contract performing lab support work.

The contracting officer sent us an RFP to respond to and said they wanted to award an 8(a) procurement. My training method had worked! I had proven that if I could do it, and I could teach someone to do it, then anyone could learn to do it! Sarah had won her first contract for around $130,000 for the full-time staffed employee.

The other interns were gaining some traction, too, by receiving inquiries to their market research questions. I had become so involved in the excitement of helping them, that I stopped actively responding to solicitations.

One day, I heard a scream from my boss' office. There were 4 or 5 people gathered around her computer. They yelled for me to come, so I quickly walked over to see what all the excitement was about. It was about the third proposal I had submitted. I had totally forgotten about it.

We had submitted it from her email, and I wasn't cc'd. She had received a response a few days after submission, and she never saw it! It was in fact an award waiting for signature. We won the proposal! We were all immediately terrified because almost 2 weeks had passed since we didn't respond to the award notice. We followed up with contracting, and luckily, he had just gotten back from vacation. The contract was won as a competitive bid for around $350,000 to staff several full-time case managers working for the Army.

This is when the second shift happened for me. I thought if I could win sole sources and I could win competitive solicitations, then I would be unstoppable. I went on to win several more competitive proposals that year while continuing to work with the interns. By the time they had finished their internship, 2 out of 3 of the interns had won a sole source, and the third had come really close.

MILLION DOLLAR LIST

A lot started to change. It became very apparent that I wasn't winning by chance or luck. Even though I knew that from the beginning, others at the office became jealous of my success and tried to make light of the contracts I had won. Contracts were coming in year-round—especially during the summer months when the government needed to spend their money.

Some nights in September, I was in the office with my boss until 1:00 a.m. emailing and talking with contracting officers. I was winning competitive proposals just as much as sole sources. I had won a $4 million contract to renovate a VA hospital wing and a $1.5 million contract to lease heavy equipment to the Army Corps. Also, at this time, the interns had graduated college and moved on, which meant I had more time to spend hunting and harnessing my craft.

There was something new that came with winning all these contracts. My boss was *kind* enough to let me know that I now had to manage a lot of them. It was another freak-out moment for me. I had no idea how to manage a contract. All I knew was that it was going to take away from my time responding to market research and solicitations.

So many times, I looked around the office, and everyone was just sitting behind their computer screens "click-click-clicking" away. I would ask myself, *What the hell is everyone doing?! I have a dozen contracts happening, and now I'm going to have to start managing them myself, too?!* These were the same people who wanted to make light of my success. *Haters gonna' hate.* But that's okay. I had to *do* it all, so I got to *learn* it all.

One of the contracts I won was to provide dentists and dental assistants out of state for a Soldier Readiness Processing (SRP) event. The soldiers needed their annual health examinations, and we were to provide support for the dental side of things. We recruited the necessary dental staff, and I met them at the military base for the weekend's health screening event. It was just me, the dental staff, and some military points of contact. I had no idea what I was doing, so I did what anyone would do ... I winged it.

It ended up going fine. Our staff met with the government points of contact, and they let them know they would be working alongside government dentists and staff. Everyone worked together as a team to meet the mission of the event. We billed $66,000 for that weekend.

I came back home from that three-day event with a new perspective, being able to see these contracts are a lot more than just a piece of paper. We ended up doing 3 more of the same events over the following 6 months because it was easy for contracting to just come back to us to do the additional work. I went to all the events and learned a lot about what to do and what not to do when delivering a contract.

There were many other contracts that I was responsible for managing. I could manage a lot of them remotely from our office because they were staffing. As long as the employees we had staffed were doing their jobs with no issues, then the COR and contracting didn't really need too much from us. We had to send our monthly deliverable reports addressing what our people accomplished that month, but those reports were mostly routine.

Aside from bidding and managing contracts, my boss had me traveling and attending a lot of conferences, too. I was very busy. The conference agendas were all the same ... PowerPoint presentations, then lunch, then match-making events. I never really took a lot of value from the conferences. By the time you speak with someone, more often than not, they've already spoken with hundreds of other people.

I would approach some of the speakers and empathize that they must be tired after 2 or 3 days of the event, just to see what they would say. I received overwhelming validation on several occasions, and it became evidently clear that they didn't even want to be at the events. After that, I made a point to not spend a lot of my time going to conferences unless there were relationships there that I wanted to show my face to.

Speaking of relationships, it's also very important for me to discuss the relationship list I'd built over the last couple of years of winning. For all the contracts I had won sole sourced or competitively, I kept a list of all the people involved. I listed the contracting officers, the CORs, and any Small Business persons I worked with in the process.

I also set up searches on FBO to let me know when an opportunity came out corresponding with that person. If it was a sources sought, I would immediately pick up the phone and let them know we are interested. If it was a solicitation, I would email or call as a form of marketing and let them know we are diligently watching all opportunities coming out of their office.

At my peak, I had a list of 3 PCRs, 10 CORs, approximately 20 Contracting Officers, and 7 Small Business Representatives who I could pick up the phone and have an easy conversation with. These were people to whom I would send regular emails and make regular phone calls. I had searches set up for all of them on FBO. I would attend as many of the conferences as I could where they would be. Because of this, I had a healthy number of inbound phone calls from them and from referred contracting officials inquiring if we could perform work/respond to their solicitations on FBO.

It took me 3 years to realize that developing this list was the most important thing that I could have done. This was more important than sole sourcing. It was a million-dollar list, and it's something everyone should either begin or continue building. Don't worry if you don't have a list or know anyone yet. Just knowing that you need to have one, puts you light years ahead of so many other contractors.

From the age of 26 to 29, I personally won 32 federal contracts. The value of these contracts totaled over $15 million dollars. I went from a broke, out-of-work graduate to a very well-versed kid, selling to the federal government. I won contracts with the Army, Army National Guard, Air National Guard, Army Corps of Engineers (USACE), Customs and Border Patrol, Department of the Navy, Department of Veteran Affairs, Defense Logistics Agency (DLA), Air Force, US Army Intelligence & Security Command (INSCOM). I was also a key player in assisting others to win their contracts, and I trained 8 other colleagues to win contracts at my company.

There was certainly a lot more in my journey to capture than I could put in this book. I tried to highlight some of my challenges, and also show my growth and successes. I'm not bragging, but rather trying to inspire you! I knew absolutely nothing when I first started, and I became more successful than most, in a few short years.

I've already alluded to some of the steps that I'm going to teach you in Part 2. It's my hope that you head into the next section believing that you can win millions in federal contracts if that's really what you want.

Your story won't be like mine. You will have your own story. I haven't told you everything in my story that I'm about to show you because I didn't know all of it then. Part 2 brings together everything I learned and everything I wish I would have done, looking back. If you follow the method I'm about to show you, your success will come much quicker and you will save yourself a lot of time, money, frustrations, and distractions.

PART II

THE LEGAL MIDDLEMAN METHOD

SECTION 1

REGULATIONS

MIDDLEMAN REGULATIONS

Illegal Pass-through Scheme

Why does the legal middleman method have to exist? Why can't you just 100% sub out the job whenever and to whomever you please? Maybe you've heard somebody say that you can, but you're probably here because you realize that's incorrect information. So, we're going to make sure you understand this very well.

Alright, so when the government pumps money into small business programs by setting certain contracts aside for small businesses like Total Small Business, HUBZone, 8(a)'s, Veteran, and Women-Owned Small Business, they're doing so to nurture and cultivate the growth of these particular small business types.

But what inevitably happens is that other businesses that do not qualify for these set-asides catch the wind of this and they get jealous. And they reach out to the small business and they say something to the effect of, "Hey, you know, congrats. We see that you're a small business. Maybe you've just won your first contract or your first few. Listen, we can do all this work. We do this all the time. Let's partner together and make it easy on you. You just take a finder's fee and then we'll handle all the rest. Sound like a deal?"

At face value, this is called a pass-through scheme[1], and it's illegal unless you do it in the way that I will soon be showing you.

Illegal Pass-through Scheme

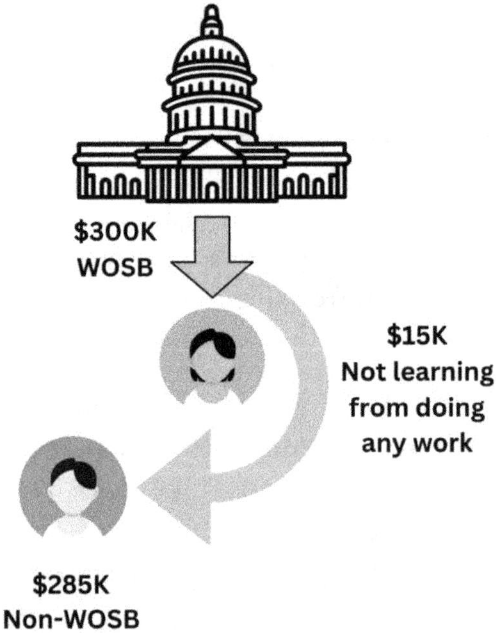

To further illustrate, here's an example of a woman-owned small business and a non-woman-owned small business. A non-woman-owned small business says, "Hey, I saw that you just won that woman-owned small business set aside contract for janitorial services for $300k. Congratulations. How about I pay you $15k free and clear, and I'll do all the work and take what's left over?"

If the WOSB is educated, she would say, "You're not a WOSB. So, I can't do that or it would be an illegal pass-through." That's without going into details because there are certain circumstances where that could happen and we're about to dive into that.

But generally speaking, are you kind of getting the point here? The illegal pass-through scheme shows $300k going toward the WOSB. But then it goes around. And only $15k sticks to the woman with a small business. And then the other $185k goes to the non-WOSB. And the WOSB doesn't learn anything because she's not doing any of the work. So, her business is not growing or expanding as intended with the use of the set-aside.

The woman-owned small business is not being supported the way that it's supposed to, and this is why it's super important that you understand what the legal pass-through scheme looks like so that you can understand how to do a legal middleman and you don't fall into the illegal portion of things.

Full and Open (Unrestricted)

Now, since this started happening more and more, the government needed to do something about it. They decided to create a governing regulation to manage this called the Limitations on Subcontracting (LOS)[2].

If at this point, you're saying to yourself, *What the heck, Derek? How am I supposed to do this? I thought this was what the whole method was about.* Just stay with me and let me show you how.

First off, the government said that Limitations on Subcontracting only applies to small business program contracts.

So, it doesn't apply to Full and Open contracts, also known as unrestricted contracts. These contracts are not bound by Limitations on Subcontracting (LOS). Many contracts are listed as full and open/unrestricted, and LOS does not apply to them. That means for contracts that are not set aside for small businesses, you can legally run the project however you want, including finding a subcontractor to do 100% of the work while you manage it.

So, full and open (unrestricted) contracts are the first opportunity for Legal Middlemanning to become aware of.

Below the SAT

At a certain point, regulators decided that below a certain value, the contract was too small to be worth placing these limits of subcontracting on. It was a bit too tedious. For example, it doesn't make sense to spend $50k to procure a contract that's $100k. Doesn't make sense, right?

So, for these small-dollar value contracts, they decided to use a simpler method because of the cost. They said for these smaller-dollar contracts, we will be using a simpler method called Simplified Acquisition Procedures (SAP)[3]. This bar was called the Simplified Acquisition Threshold (SAT), and it's currently set at $250k and is subject to future change.

This applies in 2 ways:

-For small business set-aside contracts, LOS does not apply to contracts under the SAT. So, you can subcontract small business set-aside contracts any way you like below $250k.

-For socio-economic set-aside contracts including 8(a), WOSB, VOSB, and HUBZone, limits on subcontracting do still apply regardless of the contract dollar value.

So, as you can see, everything between $0 and $250k that is a set-aside for small businesses is too small to matter. This means under this condition that you are also not bound by LOS, and you can work with a subcontractor to fulfill this work 100% within this range.

Hopefully, now things are starting to come together, and we're just getting started ...

Just keep in mind, contracts that have the socio-economic category set-aside (rather than just a small business set-aside only), including 8(a), WOSB, VOSB, and HUBZone, LOS does apply regardless of contract dollar value.

Above the SAT

Alright, so this becomes okay when it's under this bar. Now, what about everything that's above the bar? Okay, stay with me here. So, everything that is above the $250k (SAT) DOES matter that's set aside for small businesses. This is important. They said everything that's above the bar, you have to do a minimum percentage of the work, including the socio-economic categories of 8(a), WOSB, VOSB, and HUBZone, too.

That way, when you perform a minimum percentage of the work, at least X amount of money, for example, goes to a woman-owned small business, or 8(a), HUBZone, or Veteran for example. You get the point, right? They determined the minimum self-performance percentage for professional services to be 50%, and then for construction, it has to be 15%.

In this example, with a janitorial contract being $300k for the woman with a small business, now she has to do 50% of the job to meet the limits on subcontracting (LOS) because this is over the simplified acquisition threshold and the contract no longer qualifies for simplified acquisition procedures.

In this instance, 50% is $150k of the work that needs to be self-performed, and then she can sub out the rest which is another $150k to the non-WOSB, or whoever she wants because she's met her self-performance limitations.

And at this point, you might be saying, *Well, that kind of sucks that contracts over the SAT you have to self-perform 50%, and that's not really a full middleman play*. I got you. There is one exception.

Regulations say it's okay if you subcontract to another company that shares the same small business program status as you because then the money is still going where it's supposed to go to support small businesses. That actually makes sense. With our woman-owned example, that means if she works with another certified WOSB and it becomes WOSB-to-WOSB, then that's called working with a Similarly Situated Entity, and that's okay, too.

So, if a WOSB wins the contract and then they give the entire contract to another WOSB, is the money going where it's supposed to go? Yes, it is. It's going to support WOSBs. This becomes the exception because limitations on subcontracting states the prime contractor will not pay more than X amount of the money paid by the government to subcontractors that are not similarly situated. So, when it's over $250K, we will just stick with subs that are similarly situated.

Again, what does it mean to be similarly situated? It means sharing the same small business program status. In reality, teaming with a similarly situated entity will work best when you are working with a small business set-aside contract only because you will have many more options to choose other small business subcontractors that will not be in competition with you.

If you are trying to develop a teaming relationship as a WOSB with another WOSB, they are just going to cut you out of the contract and bid it directly. They don't need you. Working with small business subcontractors who aren't familiar with government contracting creates a non-competitive symbiotic relationship where both small businesses are being supported and both entities are providing value to the contract.

FAR Part 13.5

FAR Part 13.5[4] authorizes the use of simplified acquisition procedures on certain contracts that are greater than $250k up to $7.5 million. It raises the bar of the SAT up to $7.5M when in effect, which means you can do whatever you want with everything underneath because then they're saying everything under $7.5M is too small to matter in the special context of this provision. And that's a really big deal.

So, if you do find solicitations with FAR Part 13.5 you have like a lot of space to play within as a legal middleman. And that's how some of these contractors do this for contracts that are over

$250k. And that $50k? That's for base and all option years. Not $250k per year. So, a base plus 4-option year contract maxes out at $50k per year. Say if it's a $700,000 contract over five years, they may be utilizing FAR Part 13.5 to raise this bar which gives contracting and you, the prime contractor, the room to fully legal middleman.

No Past Performance

A final note about regulations- Are you caught in the chicken and the egg game of having no past performance but needing past performance to win your first contract so that you can then gain past performance?

Okay, this is not accurate. So don't worry. FAR 15.305[5] states the evaluation of a contract shall take into account past performance information regarding predecessor companies, key personnel, and subcontractors that will perform major or critical aspects of the requirement.

For legal middlemanning, it's great news that we're able to literally use our subcontractor's past performance.

But if for whatever reason you find yourself in that situation, you will not be evaluated favorably or unfavorably for not having past performance. So that means you'll get a neutral rating at worst if you don't have past performance.

It's not more complicated than this, this is all you need to hear. Whoever kind of started this chicken and the egg thing did everyone a lot of disservice, especially those who want to legally middleman.

Summary

In summary, here are the 4 regulatory methods an stances you can give 100% of a contract to for a subcontra fulfill while you solely manage the contract:

Method 1 - If the contract is full and open (unrestricted), meaning a large contract or one that is not set-aside for small business, then you can legally middleman the contract.

Method 2 - If the contract is below the Simplified Acquisition Threshold (SAT) ($250K), and set-aside for small business, you can essentially do whatever you want in the context of subcontracting.

Method 3 - If the contract is above the SAT, you can work with a similarly situated entity. Work preferably on total small business contracts where you can work with a sub that is also a total small business (similarly situated entity) so that you share that small business program.

Method 4 - If you find a special situation with FAR Part 13.5 where you can 100% sub out the contract up to the raised bar of $7.5 million, then you can legally middleman the contract.

No Past Performance- You do not need past performance to get started. You are able to use your subcontractor's (teaming partner's) projects as past performance.

SECTION 2

OFFER

AGENCY

Let's talk about agency. Agency defined is a business or organization established to provide a particular service, typically one that involves organizing transactions between two other parties.

We are in the agency business and you are going to be an agency owner. You're building a GovCon Agency and we're doing this using the Legal Middleman Method. And as you know, this means you will be bidding to win contracts. So, you will be able to manage the subcontractors as well as manage the communication with the government customer to maintain quality service.

So, our two parties that are managing this transaction are the subs and then the end user—the government. Make sense?

You are an agency owner. Congratulations! I don't know if anybody's told you this or not. Your goal as an agency owner is to start building your book of business of service contracts. We will get started with an example as an agency owner to demonstrate what building a book of business can realistically look like for your agency over time.

Example 1

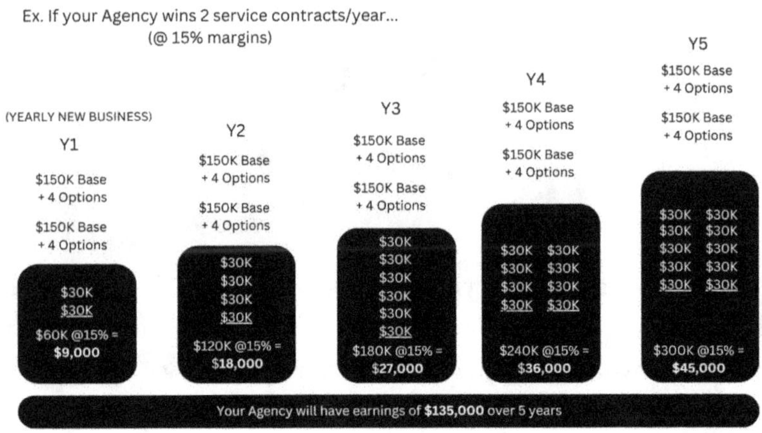

Let's suppose your agency wins two service contracts per year at approximately 15% margins, which is an average margin. And let's say the two contracts are $150k each, and they are a base plus four option years.

Each year we're adding two contracts, so this represents the set of $30k numbers that are building each year. By year 5, you'll have 10 contracts on the books. The way this looks in terms of numbers is $60k in revenue the first year, $120k in revenue the second year because it's compounding, then $180k, $240k, and then $300k by year five.

You can run the same math for the profit using 15% margins starting out at $9k for year one, $18k for year two, and so on, reaching $135k combined profit over five years. I don't know about you, but I would like to make more money than that. So, let's look at another example.

Example 2

So, let's build on this, okay? Let's say each year, the contracts that you win lead to one additional contract from organic growth (we will cover organic growth more in a future section).

This is a very common concept of organic growth. Once you get your foot in the door, once you win your first or your first couple, those contracts can lead to more contracts just through relations. We don't want to be too aggressive in our forecast because I want to give you something realistic. So, we'll just say it leads to one each year okay? So now, we're adding three contracts each year.

So now, instead of having ten contracts on the books by year 5, just through this, we have fifteen contracts by year five. And the exciting thing is that the previous contracts continue to bill out over subsequent years in addition to the new contracts that you win! That's the really cool part of this compounding and how it stacks.

These modifiers can really make the numbers scale because of this compounding. When you make little adjustments an inch at a time, over time, they become a mile. If you sway just a little over time, it's going to make a big impact. And that's what I'm trying to show you visually with this example.

Earnings Multipliers

What's allowing the powerful compounding to take place is the organic growth multiplier. There are more multipliers as well, so let's look at some others.

Multiplier #1 You could win more than two contracts a year through bidding. That's totally possible. And you could win even more than that, but let's stay conservative.

Multiplier #2 You could have higher margins, right? Let's stay with 15% because that's an average. For example, on best-value contracts, the government doesn't typically award to the lowest price. They want to award to a higher, more dependable quality service, full well knowing it's likely not going to be the least expensive offer. So, if you can demonstrate that you're the best value in this type of proposal, you're going to have better margins.

Multiplier #3 There may be contract modifications. Essentially, the contracts that you have ongoing year after year, contracting may add more work to those. Maybe they need to be modified because the scope needs to be built out. Contracts are not set in stone, especially over five years. Once issued, contracts can evolve over time and the contracts can get bigger over time. It becomes an art and a science learning how to work these contracts and help expand their scope over time.

Multiplier #4 You can also negotiate with the subs. Even if you take off 5% from their quote by asking for final and best offers and that gives you 5% back, now that you have the bargaining power of an award in hand, that 5% quickly adds up.

I'm going to give you some more strategies for all of these later in the training, because these earning multipliers, as I showed you, can make all the difference. So, imagine how much more you can get out of the contracts you win in the future by just rolling over some of these multipliers, modestly.

Example 3

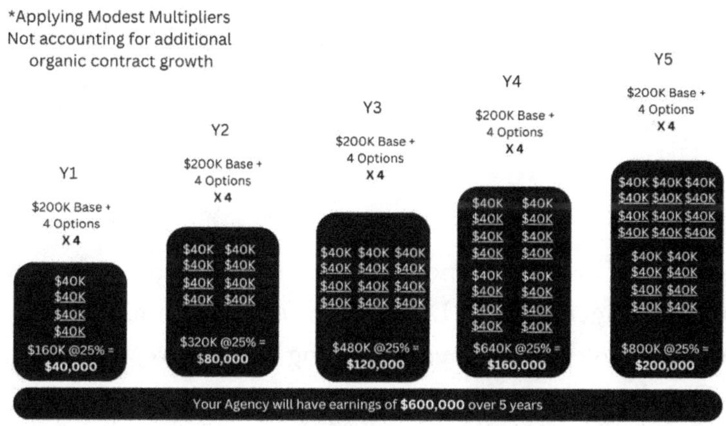

Now, in this final example, we're doing $200k instead of $150k for the contract value. We're adding a $50k bump and that's for all five years. So, as you can see it was $30k per year, and it's $40k per year. This picture I believe is very realistic for you.

Look at how it stacks now. You know how the show goes. And this example does not account for any additional organic growth of these contracts' earnings. Additional contracts are all the more reason why this is attainable.

For the numbers in year one, we're already at $160k in revenue, right? By year five, we're almost at a million in revenue ($800k). In terms of earnings, we're at $40k out of the gate for year one, then $80k, then $120k in earnings, and so on, and your agency will have earnings exceeding $600k over five years through applying some of these modest multipliers.

Isn't that crazy? It's crazy to me! I hope the visual demonstration and showing how just tweaking small things using some of these multipliers can really make a big difference.

And this is why I want you focused on service contracts as an agency owner, with a single mission to build your book of business.

Real Estate Agency

Being in the GovCon Agency game is very similar to being in the Real Estate Agency game. Let's switch gears and think of the real estate agent so that you have something to compare with being a GovCon Agency owner.

Real estate agents start with nothing. They have imposter syndrome. Real estate agents haven't sold a house until they've sold a house. What makes them legitimate? You know, they have business cards and that's it. Most agents don't even have a personal website, they use the broker's website when they first get started. Maybe they have brochures, but they start literally with not much more than a state license.

Next. Real estate agents submit offers and make deals. They are playing the numbers game.

Also, agents work under a broker who pays them commission, right? But then they get the support of having somebody to have their back, look over their shoulder on deals, and make sure they're doing it right, especially at the beginning.

Agents will sell a house that's a hundred grand, but they'll also sell a house that's a million. They're not discriminative about the dollar amount, they want as many good deals as they can find. They want as much good business as they can get.

The longer they're in the game, the more money real estate agents make. Real estate agents are not necessarily making a lot of money in year one. But they're going to make more money the longer they're in the game. And that's the point. It can be a very lucrative career. Or they can make no money.

It's totally up to the real estate agent, and it's going to depend on how active they are. Are they doing the right things? Are they following the processes? Or are they not? I'm sure we all know agents who made no money and dropped out of it. And then we may know a few agents who are absolutely killing it.

Now, let's examine the similarities as a GovCon Agency owner:

You, too, are literally starting with nothing.

You need to submit bids to win just like agents have to submit offers on houses from clients to make deals happen.

You don't have a broker but you have me, right? And cool. You don't have to pay me commissions!

You can and will have contracts for $100K, but also everything in between up to a million and more.

You're not discriminative either about the dollar values. The longer you're in this game, the more money you're also going to make as we've demonstrated.

This can also be a very lucrative long-term opportunity for an Agency owner.

Since this is your business, you can also make no money. Just like the real estate agent, it's up to you.

Are you going to put in the work? Are you going to follow the processes or are you not?

This is your invitation to step into being an agency owner. If no one's told you before, congratulations! And now you are.

DEAL OR NO DEAL?

We've been hinting at it, so let's talk about what makes a good deal or what makes a bad deal. And it's not necessarily a bad deal, but a deal that may not be a good fit for us, but may be a good fit for someone else.

Once you find bids that are a match that you want to go after on the surface level, it's extremely important to develop an approach to sort the "good" from the "bad." You want to create a shortlist. If you don't, you will either be responding to all of them, which will not be humanly possible as a very small team of 1, 2, or 3, *or*, you will not have an effective way of differentiating between the different solicitations, This will leave you vulnerable to spending part of the time trying to respond to bids you shouldn't, and then missing opportunities that would be a better match for your small business.

Perhaps, the best place to go from here is to define "good" and bad," and we can start saying "Deal" or "No Deal."

What are some of the characteristics of a Deal? As you start doing this on your own, you are going to create your own way by default. My goal is to influence your way to be one that saves you a bit more time and frustration because this could feel overwhelming at first.

Top 10 Deal Characteristics

Here are the Top 10 Characteristics of a solicitation that should influence your decision of whether something is a Deal or not.

Characteristic #1: Due Date. The due date listed on the description page of SAM.gov is the date offers are due. No later offers are accepted, ever. It's very helpful in determining a Deal to know how much time you have to put your competitive solicitation response (proposal) together.

For beginners, I recommend at least 1.5 to 2 weeks' time. If something is due in less than a week, it's unlikely you will have the chops to get pricing from subs and formulate a competitive proposal response. As you improve, you can narrow this window. The weighting of the due date window will also be impacted by how much other work you're taking on at that time as well. As a quick reference, if you have at least 1.5-2 weeks before the due date, it's possibly a Deal. Less time than that, maybe a No Deal.

Characteristic #2: Set-aside. Does the set-aside prevent you from bidding on it? If the solicitation is a set-aside for 8(a), you must be 8(a) to bid on it. Not the sub. You! If it's a set-aside for Veterans (VOSB), then you must be a VOSB or you cannot bid on it. End of story. Set-aside is a quick and powerful filter for determining Deals from No Deals.

Characteristic #3: NAICS code. NAICS code is an interesting characteristic. If you are responding to a solicitation, you want to make sure to add whatever NAICS code that is to your SAM.gov entity profile. These codes are fluid; however, they are not concrete. You do select one primary NAICS code when you first set up and register your business, and that doesn't change.

But all the other NAICS codes that you add to your profile are done at your will and reflect your company's capabilities at that time. They will, and should, change and evolve over time with your business. If your opportunity has NAICS codes different from what you already have listed, update your registration with the new code if you decide to mark it a Deal.

Also, each NAICS code is associated with a Size Standard. As your business grows and you gain revenue under certain NAICS codes, this can become more impactful to your decision-making. The Size Standard reflects the trailing average of revenue over the last 3 years that your company shall not exceed or else it will temporarily lose its' small business size standard under that NAICS code.

This would make you a non-small business for that NAICS code or codes, so you would not be able to bid on solicitations that are set aside for that code. If you find yourself in this situation, you will need to bid on contracts under different NAICS codes until your annual revenues dip back below the threshold and return you to a state of being considered a small business. It's a bigger conversation, but I want to at least expose you to this concept if you find yourself winning many contracts in a concentrated area.

Characteristic #4: Site Visit. Site visits are sometimes mandatory. If it is mandatory and you don't attend (or can't), you will be precluded from bidding. Watch for "mandatory" language, or to see if you've even missed a visit date as this can dramatically influence between a Deal or a No Deal. If a site visit is not mandatory but you or your subcontractor is unable to attend, you may want to consider a No Deal, depending on how complicated the work is to be done.

Characteristic #5: Geography. How does the geographical location of the work compare to where your small business is located? For construction and construction-related industries, this can be a significant factor. So much so, that contracting may indicate for a construction project that the business be within an X-mile radius of the place of performance in order to bid on it.

I do recommend single-trade construction as part of our Industry Reports, but it's not likely you will come across this often. And for all the other services listed, you are free to provide support with subcontractors that are local to the area, regardless of where your small business resides.

This often becomes more of a question of what the small business owner is comfortable with. What are you comfortable with? Are you comfortable working within all 50 states, or do you want to work within a tri-state area to get started? Ask this question to yourself, and use the answer to help shape your Deal or No Deal criterion.

Characteristic #6: Scope of work. What is the scope of work? Meaning, what actually needs to be accomplished by the contract? Some work is more specialized than others. Larger requirements can require multiple trades or subs to accomplish the vastness of scope. Are there special requirements or cautions associated with the scope, like environmental or safety factors? Becoming clear on what the scope of work really entails can influence a Deal or a No Deal, depending on what you're prepared to manage and expose your small business to.

Characteristic #7: Pricing. A lot goes into pricing. From a Deal or No Deal standpoint, we can consider how the government is asking us to present our pricing, and if that is something that we will be able to get the subcontractor to quote in accordance with. Also, if the government provides a Rough Order of Magnitude (ROM) or dollar value range of what they think the job should cost, are you in the same ballpark? Other considerations include an incumbent contract value if this same job has been serviced by a contractor in the past (maybe even still currently).

Pricing decision-making is something that you want to start considering from the beginning because it heavily weights your Deal or No Deal. You can start by reviewing Pricing CLINS or any pricing spreadsheet supplied with the solicitation document and by also submitting questions (RFIs) to contracting to help influence your Deal or No Deal decision and pricing calculations.

Characteristic #8: Proposal. What is required in your proposal response to the government as requested in the solicitation? Good question! Isn't this something you want to know the answer to before you get in too deep? I think so. It could be a straight RFQ (Request for Quote) response consisting of filling out the SF1449 form and pricing only, or it can be a full-blown RFP (Request for Proposal) that will require you to provide a mix of technical proposal information, past performance information, and pricing breakdowns.

One isn't necessarily good or bad. The golden question is do you want to put this response together, or even more so, are you able to put the response together as a competitive offer? Once again, the due date will influence the proposal assembly time factor. But also, do you have the technical write-ups, or are you able to get them from the subcontractor to formulate a compliant proposal response?

In an RFP, you can be asked for technical information like resumes, staffing plan/approach, quality control plan, key personnel, project milestones, your plan to meet the requirements of the statement of work, and so much more. When looking at a solicitation, find this information quickly to gauge, what, and if, this is something you want to put together and are able to put together to further inform a Deal or No Deal decision.

Characteristic #9: Evaluation. Similar to proposal criteria, what does the winning bid look like and is it something you think you can be competitive with? The two most common evaluation strategies are Lowest Price Technically Acceptable (LPTA) and Best Value.

LPTA is often used for commodity items and services where the government has high confidence that the approach or end product is going to be very similar, if not exact. You further see this with terminology like "name brand or equal." In an LPTA procurement, the government does not have a lot of questions about what they're going to be getting, so their perceived risk is low. For that reason, they can go with the lowest bidder (that meets the minimal qualifying criteria that deem a company to be technically acceptable).

Best value evaluations are higher risk. There is potentially more interpretation as to how the work can be performed. This can also be higher visibility projects or projects that more greatly affect their respective mission. In other words, the government can't afford for the project to get messed up. It's a higher risk. And for that reason, the government wants to see more information than pricing to qualify contractors.

Again, this will consist of more robust technical information and past performance information on the company or the teaming parties. So, once you can identify whether the solicitation is LPTA or Best Value, you can decide whether this is a bid you can be competitive with or not, and that should better inform your Deal or No Deal decision.

Characteristic #10: Legal Middleman Approach. As we've discussed, what is the Legal Middleman Approach you're going to take on this? Is it a full and open contract? Is it below the SAT as a small business contract? Do you plan to work with an SSE above the SAT? Or maybe you've found a FAR Part 13.5 where the SAT is raised?

You will get faster at answering these questions through reading, researching, and asking key questions. And to get started, since most of the subs you are working with will likely be small businesses, you can focus more on small business set-aside contracts to guarantee an SSE relationship no matter what, and open up to the other methods from there.

A couple more notes on these characteristics overall. I've hinted that some of the factors may have more weight to influence your Deal or No Deal decision-making more than others. You will grow into and find what's most important to you. You may develop a ranking system or a points-based system, or you may operate more from the gut with these 10 Characteristics. Whatever works for you, works for me because I want this to be your system.

A second note is that once you decide that something is a Deal, that doesn't mean a deal can't fall apart. Deals fall apart all the time in all industries. Ever make a bid on a house that doesn't pass inspection? Once a subcontractor walks the site and starts putting numbers together, they may back out.

If you find yourself with no way to quote or the sub is too afraid to quote because they don't agree with the statement of work, the deal becomes dead in the water. It's okay, it happens. Work at continually nurturing the flow of information between all parties so that the right decisions can be made as quickly as possible for everyone involved.

INDUSTRIES

Welcome to Industries. The Government Contracting arena initially hits us with these questions when we're a new government contractor as a new startup.

What's your industry? What niche do you want to be in? What do you want to sell to the government?

Have you ever been asked any of these questions? Have you ever heard this in a video? Have you ever thought of this just on your own?

Unfortunately, these can quickly lead us straight into a trap that most don't ever make it out of.

The Trap

Here's what an illustration of "The Trap" looks like and the detrimental effects it has on our small businesses when trying to enter the government contracting industry.

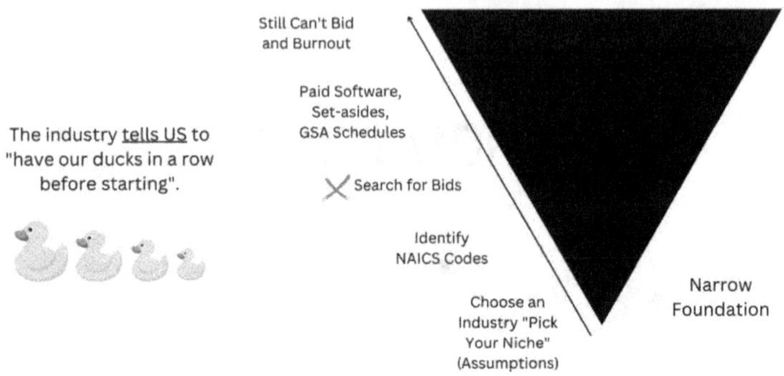

Step 1. (What NOT to do)

The industry tells us to have our ducks in a row before starting. When I'm saying industry here, I'm referencing the government contracting industry as a collective. "Have your ducks in a row before starting." This is what we're told. And what this process looks like early on is to choose an industry or pick your niche, right? And you do this based on assumptions. This is the first thing you're told to do. Again, what do you want to sell to the government?

Step 2. (What NOT to do)

Once you do that, you're supposed to identify the NAICS codes that match up with whatever you've chosen.

Step 3. (What NOT to do)

Then start searching for bids that match the NAICS codes.

BUT what happens when we follow this formula? We get stuck, we hit a wall, and there's an X here for a reason because this is where everybody kind of falls off a cliff or hits a wall.

It's because most end up not finding the bids for the industry they chose, or they're not finding them in the way they think they should find them. Why? Because you've chosen based on a NAICS code as opposed to doing real research on the bid opportunities that correspond with those NAICS codes.

So, now we have a problem. Since there is no obvious or direct way to solve the problem, we become frustrated or feel defeated. Eventually, to try to solve that problem, we start to externally seek. Paid software, set-asides, GSA schedules, and many other things that are often flashed in front of our eyes suddenly become easy targets as to why we're not progressing. *Hmmm. Maybe relationship marketing or going to conferences was the key along...?*

No! None of these are a magic wand. If you're not finding the bids, these are not going to help you find them. None of these are going to make the perfect bids for you magically appear. And unfortunately, these can cost a lot of money, and a lot of time as a consequence, and then we eventually burn out, become cynical, and quit.

You and I both know external seeking does not address the root of any problem ... And this problem is that you're not finding bids for the industry you "chose."

This is the consequence of listening to industry tell you that you need to have your ducks in a row. And as you can tell, doing so does not result in a very solid foundation. This is a very narrow foundation. As I said, you will struggle to find bids if you approach your business this way. The underlying reason for this is there was no proof of concept first, so you are destined to hit this proverbial wall.

Good news, it's not just you and it's nearly inevitable if this is what you've been doing!

This is building on a narrow foundation. This approach forces you to make assumptions about the industry or the niche you want to go into instead of proving it first.

I'm saying it multiple times. This is what nearly everybody does. This is what we're told to do. Pick a niche. What do you want to sell to the government? Cool, then go and find it. It's backward.

This one piece of misinformation is single-handedly responsible for the failure of thousands of new GovCon Startups that never even make it to being Agency Owners.

The Solution

Now, let's have a wide foundation. No more narrow foundation. I already told you Step 1 is backward, so let's look at doing this the right way.

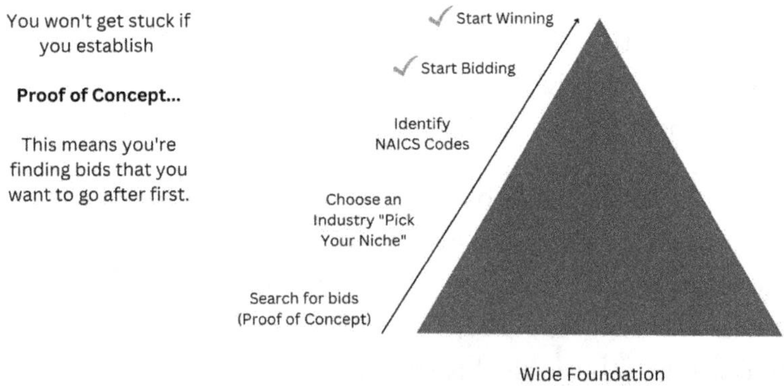

Step 1. (The right way)

Search for bids. It should be a messy process at first using various NAICS codes, PSC codes, and keywords. We don't move beyond this until we're finding bids that we're interested in until we have that proof of concept. I want you saying "Yes, that would be something I would be interested in bidding on" before you decide you're finished so that you have a strong foundation from a verified proof of concept.

If you can knock this first step out of the park, then everything else becomes easy. This "not having the ducks in a row strategy" ends up delivering the result of what people think "having their ducks in a row" will give them because now we are operating from a place of alignment.

Step 2. (The right way)

So, you search for bids first, and then you have that proof of concept. From there, you choose an industry, or you pick your niche, or niches, or industries. What? Yes, you wouldn't pick something that you weren't first finding bids for, but that's literally what they're telling us to do. Here, pick first, and then find the bids. Do you see how backward it is to do it the other way?

Step 3. (The right way)

So, we pick and it's easy. Then we just identify the NAICS codes that are in alignment with the niche, multiple niches, or industries *and* that are in alignment with the bids that we are finding.

See how smooth that is? Then what happens?

Then we don't get stuck, and we don't hit the wall. We don't have to seek externally and chase shiny objects that have nothing to actually do with the bidding procurement process. We don't have to do any of those things including investing time and the money that will have low or no return on your investment. This actually saves you so much time and literal dollars.

Step 4. (The right way)

Now what? We get to go to the next natural step and start bidding! Because guess what? We've already identified bids we are interested in. We've already found the bids. And now we're just so good to go now. We've since made the decision that this is what we want to go after because of strong alignment and we can confidently proceed with bidding.

Step 5. (The right way)

Finally, you start bidding, you start learning, and then you start winning. This is a wide foundation. You won't get stuck again if you establish this proof of concept first. It's so important. If you take one thing away from this entire section, it's proof of concept first. This means you're finding bids that you want to go after first and then backing into them. It's the most important thing because it results in alignment.

Okay. So, if you're feeling a bit anxious or you don't know if you have the confidence to do this yet, forget that. I have a thousand percent confidence in you. I've seen this time and time again, and you're going to do it exactly the same way. So, just follow what I've laid out for you.

And I'm going to be making it even easier for you. I'm literally going to spoon-feed this to you.

In order to do this, we do have to move forward, though. Do I need to have the commitment from you that you're moving forward? You're not going to stay stuck in paralysis analysis and posture syndrome. You're not saying *I don't know what I want to sell to the government* because we're not going to operate from that inverted triangle with the weak foundation anymore.

We're going to prove it first! And then once we do, we have to move forward. The best way to get started is to *get started.*

Here's a fact. You don't know what your first contract win is going to be. I think that's such a profound statement and I hope you do too. You don't know what the first bid is that you're going to win. So how can you "have your ducks in a row" and start acting and changing your business based on something that hasn't even happened yet?

There is no perfect plan in life and in business. I'm so sorry to tell those of you who are perfectionists.

It's okay, I'm a recovering perfectionist myself. We like to plan things and have this perfect plan, but man plans and God laughs.

It's not the way it works in reality. Only someone who's been through it can tell you that you can have the best ducks lined in a row, the best business plan, and the best whatever. Then there's reality.

We don't want to live in fantasy land. We don't want to live in dreamland. We don't want to live in theory. We want to live in reality. Practical things that you can actually do or that you can control shape your destiny, and the real results have real causes and effects, right?

I'll show you later on, but you don't want to be romantic about the industry so much. I want to plant this seed right now. Do not romanticize the industry. You want to romanticize the bid or the deal. Okay, is it a good bid or a bad bid? Is it a good deal or a bad deal? That's what's important. Not what flavor of the week it is.

Remember the real estate agents. They will sell a house in the country or in the city. They'll sell a house that's $100k or that's $1 million, right? They're not picky per se. They're an agent. You're an agency. You need to start thinking along these terms. It's really going to benefit you if you do.

Industry Reports

So, I told you I was going to help you. I created an Industry Report. And right now, I've analyzed eight industries, and this may evolve over time, but these high-demand service industries are great to legal middleman specifically for federal contracting. This way you don't have to romanticize deals and you also have a variety to choose from based on what aligns best with your business to get started.

I've scraped all the NAICS codes. I've written brief reports on how these industries are thriving in federal contracting, so I've made it super easy for you to just kind of plug and chug and start moving forward with one or two or all of these industries.

I'm truly okay with wherever you want to go from here. You can do stuff aside from this if you want, but I didn't want to just leave you here saying, "Okay. Derek said I need to get started. I need to move forward with a niche or an industry or whatever." Again, that's not what I'm saying, but I *am* saying you've got to move forward with something. So, I'm giving you something to move forward with.

So, if you're interested, you can download the "8 High-Demand Industries for Legal Middlemanning" industry report here: legalmiddleman.com/industryreport[6].

PROOF OF CONCEPT

Let's get aligned. We've already talked about alignment being the most important thing that will make everything flow so much easier and keep you from hitting the proverbial wall. In order to have alignment, we said we have to have Proof of Concept.

So, let's take a minute to get you running in this direction with what you currently offer as a Legal Middleman or what you think you want to offer. By the end of this, you will either be supported in your existing offer or you will be made aware of other more supported opportunities.

Alignment Exercises- Strategic Searches on SAM.gov

If you've watched any of my SAM.gov Bids LIVE episodes on YouTube, this is the exact search I use to search and find opportunities for the show. The Middleman search should open you to a lot of possibilities and opportunities—some you may have never known or considered.

Based on this search, what are you seeing that you would be interested in going after? What are you finding where there are multiples of bids that you would be able to build a pipeline out of and play the numbers game with?

Once you get some answers to these questions, you can start to see if they fall into the 8 in-demand service industries (if you're using that resource), or if you want to carve out an additional industry for something different.

Legal Middleman Expanded Search Exercise

Response Date: Next Month

Notice Type: Both Solicitation, and Combined Synopsis/ Solicitation

NAICS: 236, 237, 238, 517, 518, 519, 541, 561, 621, 721, 484, 485, 491, 492, 493, 622, 562

Set-asides: Total Small Business, and any set-asides your Small Business currently has like 8(a), HUBZone, WOSB, and VOSB

See the screenshot for an example of what this search should look like.

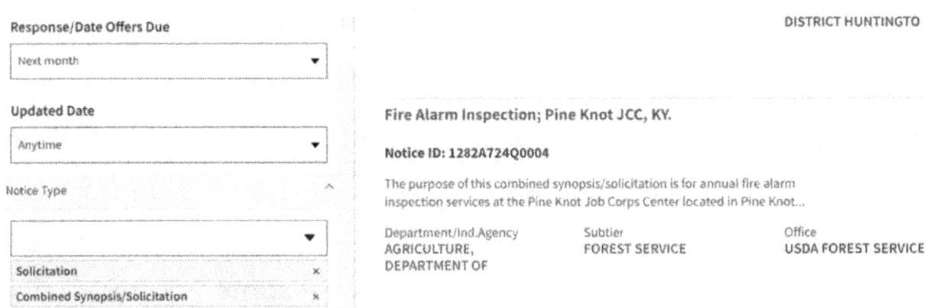

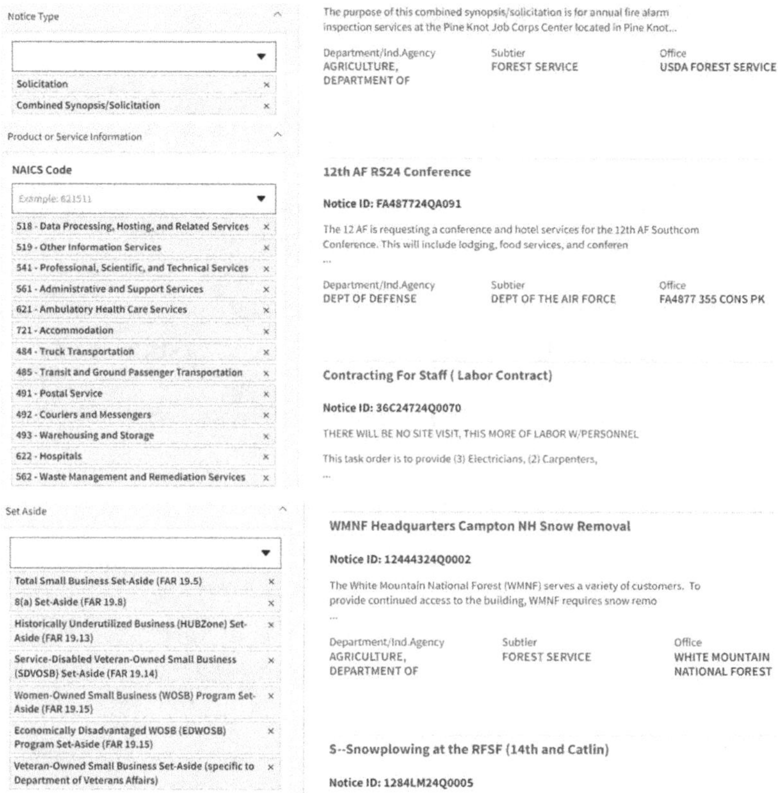

Now, let's say as an example after conducting the Legal Middleman search, you find you are interested in grounds maintenance opportunities, so you would like to try to double-down on those bid opportunities.

Great! Here is a search using the industry report information for grounds maintenance. This will clean up the search results and put many of the grounds maintenance opportunities in front of you that are live Solicitations that you can actually bid on and for responses that are due over the next 30 days.

Legal Middleman Focused Search Exercise

Response Date: Next Month

Notice Type: Both Solicitation, and Combined Synopsis/ Solicitation

NAICS: 561730, 561710, 561790, 238990

Set-asides: Total Small Business, and any set-asides your Small Business currently has like 8(a), HUBZone, WOSB, and VOSB

See the screenshot for an example of what this search should look like.

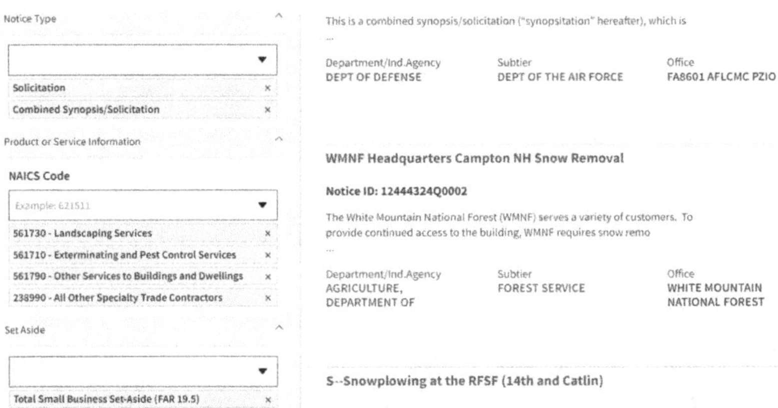

Calibrate

You will want to apply these proof-of-concept exercises throughout the year on as many potential industries that you become curious about. You should never stop searching, there is no "set it and forget it." We don't want to make assumptions, we want to prove it. If it's not there, there is no magic wand that can put it there.

To fully apply this, calibrate your searches quarterly. As you get better at this, you can also adjust your searches. One adjustment you can make is opening up the response date from next month to the next 3 months.

You can also adjust the notice type to include sources sought and pre-solicitation. This will result in opening up your forecasts so you can see opportunities coming down the pipeline from earlier stages. I only recommend you do the latter, however, after 6 months, or after winning your first (or first couple) awards. The most important thing at the very beginning is to be focused and I don't want you at risk of being distracted by opportunities that you can't bid on yet like sources sought and pre-solicitation.

UMBRELLA STRATEGY

I use this example often, but it isn't meant to pick on the particular service. Let's use Notary Services as our example here.

I often hear that small business owners want to offer Notary Services to the government. Why? Because they are already a certified Notary Public, and now they want to offer their services to the government. Stop immediately. This is the trap! Do you see that this way of thinking comes from the inverted triangle shake foundation?

If the research is done first, you'll find there aren't a lot of Notary Services opportunities to bid on in SAM.gov. The government is not buying a lot of it. So, if you wanted to build an entire federal contracting business by offering notary services, you would likely not survive. There's just not enough to go around.

Here's the point. Is it wrong to offer notary services? No, of course not. Fully depending on this one weak leg of a stool to prop your entire business is reckless. After being active in federal contracting for a decade now, and working with hundreds—if not thousands—of new federal contractors at this place in time, I've seen new federal contractors fall into the trap, hit the proverbial wall, and not generate any sort of proof of concept.

So, now I'm happy to be able to provide one more solution to your offer and the way your business approaches federal contracting as a legal middleman. I call this approach the Umbrella Strategy.

In our example of notary services, Notary Services could form one prong of the umbrella. But what else can fit under the umbrella as a similar or even complementary service? Maybe something like courier services. There are also types of staffing like front desk and administrative support. Or perhaps just other professional services that require specialized credentials similar to notary services, like court reporting and paralegal.

If you have something that you do self-perform like notary services, how can you build out your offer horizontally to be something that is more diversified that services as additional prongs under your umbrella and is also aligned with what the government is buying so that you can bid year-round and play the numbers games in alignment?

Think of each solicitation listed on SAM.gov as a problem the government needs to have solved. How can you best position your offer to solve many problems instead of only one for the government? In other words, if a contracting officer called you one day because they saw that you have a certain NAICS code in your SAM.gov profile and they wanted to know if you could perform this other similar service, would you say "No" because it's not in your exact capabilities? Or would you say Yes and rise to the occasion?

I hope you see that this Umbrella Strategy as part of legal middlemanning allows you a vehicle to creatively solve many of the government's problems.

Once you build out the prongs of your umbrella to include one, two, or three other similar services, you have to tie it all together as an overarching umbrella that presents your company and what you offer. It's easy to say you're a notary services company when that's all that you offer. But then there's not much opportunity there with the government if that's all you do.

But what about our example of offering notary, admin, court reporting, and paralegal? You could make the argument that you are a "Professional Services" company that offers a variety of credentialed personnel to support the government's various key missions. That sounds pretty good. Be creative and figure out how you can tie your services together as one unified offer so you can put it on a capability statement, your website, or even your business card.

You can check out more Umbrella Strategy examples at www.legalmiddleman.com/umbrella.[7]

SECTION 3

SUBCONTRACTORS

MARKUPS

So, let's take a look at sub markup, and I'm going to explain to you what I mean by this. The sub is going to submit their quote to you. This should go without saying, but just for anybody who doesn't understand. You're not going to take what the sub gives you and submit it directly to the government. You have to do your own markup on top of it, of course. And with that being said, you're not going to tell the sub anything. You want to build profit and costs into your markup.

You're going to add your expenses and profit onto the quote that the sub submits to you with their proposal. So, let's just look at a quick example of profit and costs.

Costs Example

You can have direct costs and indirect costs. For direct costs, you have your subs quote, let's say it's a $100k just to use round numbers. And let's say you have $10K in direct costs in expenses for travel. Okay. So, that's $110k. And then let's just say you have some indirect costs of $5,000 for overhead to manage the project. So, your total direct and indirect costs are $115k.

Now, you need to do a 15% profit markup. So, we'll just add the 15% to that. That will land us at $132,250, resulting in a profit of

$ 17,250. If you know you're trying to work towards a $15-20K profit on this project, you can do the simple math to see approximately what your markup should be, and then evaluate if that is a competitive and realistic margin.

And this is what your breakdown would look like from a basic high-level view. Although these are just the basics, your pricing breakdowns should not be overly complicated for the service contracts that you're going after.

For this example, it can be good to add travel because you want to go visit the site a couple of times. If you win the contract, it's good for relationship building and quality control, et cetera, you know, go and surprise the sub or whatever. It's good to build in costs like this, but it's entirely up to you. It also just depends on the requirements of the contract and what you feel comfortable with.

Ranges

I will share with you some generally accepted markup ranges that you can use as guides as a prime contractor to add to your subcontractor costs.

For lowest price contracts (LPTA), competitive margins are going to be around 5-20%. That's on top of what the sub is sending to you. Like the example we just went through, that's why I use 15% as an example. Your markup is going to consist of your profit and costs.

For best-value contracts, it's more like 10- to 35% markup ranges. Again, these are not set in stone, but these are competitive ranges.

You can certainly go higher. Just know that the higher you're going to go, the less competitive you're eventually going to be.

Best-value contracts, for example, are not only concerned about the price. They're often just as much concerned about the non-price factors like your proposal, your past performance, and your overall approach of how you're going to complete the work. So, you can justify charging higher margins for best-value contracts because it's not the only factor that is being evaluated.

Every bid is different and your approach for every contract should be based off of identifying what a competitive winning strategy is going to be, and we will talk more about that in the proposal writing phases.

I'm simply giving you ranges here. They are here to give you some close ballpark figures. Don't just take anything blindly—even what I give you. You have to take everything with a small grain of salt and apply it to the actual contract that you're looking at.

Earnings Multipliers

I'm going to share more about Earnings Multipliers in a future section, but I at least wanted to let you know that there are these ways to be more profitable in contracts besides the profit that you charge in case these ranges have you feeling a little underwhelmed.

Earnings Multipliers exist that allow you to be more profitable on the back end of the contract so that your margins to the government and overall costs remain within the competitive range. For example, let's say you're at 15% profit markup, but then you can save another 5% on the contract from negotiating with your sub. Well, now your profitability just increased from 15- to 20%. It doesn't mean you're charging the government a total of 20%, but your overall profitability has increased through better business management.

We will talk about these different earning multipliers so it doesn't have to all be on the front end. We will discuss lifetime value of the contract, and organic growth, and other tangible things you can do to realistically squeeze the most juice from the lemon.

IGCE

Many things that we discuss can come into play with what your margins are too, so there is one other factor that I wanted to mention called the independent government cost estimate (IGCE).

The IGCE is like the number the government has written down on a secret napkin with what they think the job should cost. The government has already done its estimation process of what they think this should cost, and so they're willing to allow a margin above or below what they think it should be. They're going to have their own range, and they're going to have their own number and their own ballpark.

It's not going to affect your margins directly, but for example, I had a client who was bidding on a contract and their number was way lower than what the government was showing in the range that was provided. (The government doesn't always share the range, but they did on this solicitation.)

First, I told my client to go back and check to make sure both they and their sub hadn't missed anything in the scope. Once that was confirmed to be clear, they needed to increase their price because they were going to be very far outside of the government's range to the point where their pricing would be considered unreasonable or unbalanced.

I'm highlighting the story to demonstrate how margins can be affected by what the government thinks the project could cost. If you're in this game long enough, you will find that this is one of the ways the government can influence your pricing. I'm just trying to arm you with some of these stories and plant seeds now because you're not going to run into all of this at once. You will eventually encounter all of it, and so much more, so then it won't be the first time you're experiencing it.

Competition

What are competing bidders charging? This also affects the competitive play. Pricing isn't only influenced by what the government thinks it should be calculated at, but it can also be influenced by what the competitive bidders are charging.

Now, of course, if multiple bidders show up everybody's outside the acceptable range, then contracting can cancel the requirement and do a re-recompete. But if that happens, maybe the government missed something. Maybe industry is trying to tell the government something like, "No, this is actually what the market going rate is," so that is also going to affect things.

What about incumbent pricing established by the company that's already providing this service? We always want to ask contracting if there is an incumbent providing this service and what the existing award number is. You also need to ask about the existing dollar value of the contract. This way you can try to ballpark and back into competitive markups.

Also, look for ways the competition is using technological advancements to be more competitive and how they are anticipating inflation for long-term contracts to price option years. You can even look to the commercial space for proof of this. Everything affects everything in the market economy, so always be thinking about how you can best utilize resources to make a more competitive play than the competition, or at the very least, learn from those who are already doing it.

RULE OF 2

A quick word to the wise with the rule of two, specifically when it comes to subs quoting work for you.

Make sure you get at least two sub quotes, okay? This ensures quote accuracy through comparison, meaning if you get one quote, you have no way of gauging if it's high, low, or exact because you have nothing to compare it to.

If you're an expert in a particular field, that would be one of the rare occasions where it could be possible. But in all these other instances when you are doing a legal middleman scenario, you're not going to be an expert. You want to get at least two quotes.

You're not going to know what it should actually cost. So, you're going to be reliant on a sub. For that reason, you need to get multiple quotes. When I say multiple quotes, at least two, and that's why we have the rule of two.This also ensures a backup if one of your subs backs out, which may not be great, but it's better than nothing. Then you have someone to backfill them with.

As I said, you do not want to be desperate to bid on a job with only one quote. Because you can end up winning the job, and then having no way to fulfill that if the one sub backs out. But if you do have to go to the backup sub, that backup sub is possibly going to be higher than what you budgeted for from the first competitive sub that reneged. Does that make sense?

Now, where do you think that difference is going to come from if you have to go to your backup sub that is a little bit higher? That differential is going to come out of your margins, it will come out of your profit.

It could turn a profitable contract into a break-even contract, or even into a non-profitable contract—meaning you lose money on the job. This is really, really important. Unfortunately, I've seen this happen far too many times when someone just feels really comfortable with the sub, and then they get burned.

Next, the sub must quote exactly the way the government is requesting that the pricing be presented. Do not accept an all-in number from a company that's quoting this for you if the government is requesting a pricing breakdown. If you try to break it down yourself, you put yourself at risk. They must break it down the way the government asks, exactly.

Don't just accept one number from a sub and then divide it in whatever way that you think makes sense, because if something ends up happening with these pricing CLINS and they change over time, you could find yourself in a very unprofitable situation potentially.

For example, what if the government extends the pricing CLIN where you weren't making money on one pricing CLIN option, but it was okay because you were making up the money on these other very profitable pricing CLIN options? Then you can get burned. What if the government ends up needing more of one thing and less of another? You could end up going from being profitable to unprofitable.

So, if a subcontractor gives you an all-in number when the government is asking for a breakdown, you can say, "Thank you for giving me this, but I need you to break this down because it's going to live throughout the life of the contract, and situations can arise where we need the breakdown."

Lastly, do not let a sub sweet talk you. Actions speak louder than words. And boy, oh boy, is that no truer than when it comes to government contracting. Actions speak way louder than words. If the sub is saying all the right things to you, but they're not providing you with what you've specifically asked for in the quote, this is a warning sign. You need to communicate with them. You need to re-engage with them and figure out what's going on.

You can say, "Thank you. However, I need this." Now, if they keep putting you off but are saying all the right things like, "We're going to give you the best price" or "We do this all the time", and it's not followed up with action, it's a cause for concern.

And before too many of these happen, you'll want to move on from them. And if they are the only sub that you have, for example, and you can't reach the Rule of 2, then this becomes a No Deal because you cannot rely on them. You need to have multiple quotes—especially when you're working with subs that are exhibiting some form of warning signs or red flags.

In summary, we would rather have no business over a bad business. This is a short lesson, but it is so important. I always tell everyone if you come to me and say, "Derek, I won!." I'm most likely not going to be excited.

I will get excited after the wheels are in motion because when you win, that's kind of the oh-crap moment where everything is tested and we need to make sure things are good ... The subs are good. The wheels are in motion to get this going. Then after that, we can celebrate. That's why all these things have to be in place first. Otherwise, something that should be really good, can quickly end up being something really bad and really scary.

SUBCONTRACTOR SITE VISIT CHECKLIST

Here we have a subcontractor site visit prep checklist. You can either give this to the sub, you can feel free to communicate it to them in your own way, or you can just use it as your reference for whatever you want to do. I want to keep it short and sweet but packed with the most important information that I've seen to prepare subs to go on site visits. You can download a copy of the checklist by visiting www.legalmiddleman.com/sitevisit .[8]

Site Visit Preparation

The first thing you want to do is prepare the subcontractors for the site visit. Doing so will put them in a position to get the most out of it and potentially give your team a competitive edge. Here are some items to follow for preparing for the site visit:

#1 Print a copy of the Statement of Work and any necessary drawings or photos to bring with you.

You would be surprised at how many companies show up to the site visit without this information. Sometimes, it's even the government POC who leads the site visit is the one that is underprepared. Having this with you ensures you have it at the site for your own reference, but you may also become the go-to person should a second look be needed, and you're the only one with it printed.

#2 Make sure you have base access and background check information submitted (if required).

It's very frustrating trying to bring individuals onto a base who are not on the approved list. It's a waste of everyone's time and may even blow your chances of seeing the site. Always make sure credentials are not required to enter the base, and if they are, provide them ahead of time.

#3 Sign in to the sign-in sheet for our company (in case a site visit is mandatory for us to bid).

The subcontractor shall sign in on behalf of the Prime contractor they are teaming with if the Prime contractor cannot be present. This is because sometimes site visits are mandatory, and since the Prime contractor is the one who will be submitting the bid directly to the government, you don't want your prime-sub team to be excluded from bidding on the contract because you technically didn't attend.

#4 Bring informed questions.

Just like in high school, it's always great to ask informed questions. It can set you apart from the crowd, but more importantly is that when you prepare questions ahead of time, you're much more likely to ask better questions and get better answers instead of waiting to think up questions on the spot. Start thinking about how you would approach the work and see if any approach-type questions surface.

Pay Attention During the Site Visit

Pay attention to the following items during the site visit:

#1 How many other companies are on the sign-in sheet?

Gaining this information can give you a somewhat informed idea of how much competition there will be, and who it will be.

(As the prime, you can use this information to search fpds.gov awards to see what other contracts the competitors have won.)

#2 Who from the government is in attendance (names, positions)?

This can begin to unveil the players on the government's side for this job. The person who conducts the site visit could also be the person who will be the COR (Contracting Officer's Representative) once the award is issued. In that case, it's a good person to be knowledgeable of.

#3 Is there any mention of an incumbent or existing contractor?

An incumbent contract is a company that is already doing the work and their contract is coming to an end or has recently ended. If there is an incumbent, it is highly likely their company name will be talked about by the government POC, but if they don't, it's also a good question to ask.

If you do find out who the incumbent is, you can also look at the old contract to see what the contract value is to help you ballpark the upcoming bid. If you do this, though, you will also want to try to find out if there have been any scope changes because you can't always compare an old project to a new project entirely apples-to-apples.

#4 Do they mention anything about existing problems?

This can make a significant impact on your approach to the bid. If you can speak to any existing problems they are currently facing or explain your approach to addressing them, this can go a long way towards creating a compelling offer—especially if it's a bid where the government is awarding on best overall value the offer presents. Also, simply demonstrating to the government that you fully understand the problem can make them feel heard and help them believe you are the right contractor for the job.

Post Site Visit Questions

#1 Submit your questions to us (ABC, LLC) after the site visit so we can have contracting answer your questions.

All questions must be submitted in writing from the Prime contractor to the contracting officer before the questions and answers due date. Typically, the sooner questions get submitted, the sooner they get answered and allow you to proceed with formulating your bid.

#2 Is there anything missing from the job that will prevent you from accurately quoting it?

This is really important because you're now at the stage of investing more time and resources. If there is anything new that you learned from the site visit that is making the job no longer attractive to bid, this is something that needs to be communicated to determine if there can be a workable solution with contracting or if this deal is now a No Deal.

#3 Does this have signs of being a "nightmare job" that it would be best to move on from it?

After the site visit, ask yourself if there are any signs of this project being a nightmare job. Similar to the previous point, now is the time to fully commit to the project or to reevaluate if there is cause for concern. Perhaps the project has safety issues that accompany it. Maybe what contracting is asking for is unreasonable and unattainable the way it's being presented. These are the things to get out into the open now before any further time is invested.

#4 Is there enough time to quote this job?

Simply put, after attending the site visit, is everything still on track to be able to quote by the due date, or has something new been discovered where extra time is going to be needed? If extra time is needed, communicate with us and we can request an extension of the due date for the various reasons resulting from the site visit.

For next steps, we will watch for answers to the questions to be posted and share that information once we receive it. Please begin working on the areas of the quote that you can get started on unless you're waiting on answers to questions to begin (we will discuss more). If additional questions come up, it's important to let us know asap so we can also have them submitted.

SUB SCRIPT

Teaming

The concept of working with a subcontractor to fulfill the requirements of a job together, is known as Teaming. If you win the award, you will be moving forward with a teaming agreement between your company and theirs. The difference between a straight subcontracting or outsourcing model and teaming, is that through teaming, both parties remain directly engaged in the project.

There is also a clear division of labor. Our approach consists of teaming because we are still required to be involved in the contract at all times as the prime contract holder to facilitate all communication with the government, to ensure all contract deliverables are being met, and to properly manage the subcontractor.

We are not interested in merely giving an entire contract to another company and taking a hands-off approach, only to send an invoice when it's all finished. We're not doing that. There are some in the industry that give advice that is dangerously close to this, but you won't fall prey to that now because you understand the concept of teaming that should be brought to government contracting.

GC

Once you have a solicitation that you are interested in on SAM.gov, you want to verify that you can find subcontractors as teaming partners to quote the job by running a search near the Place of Performance where the work will commence. We use Google Maps, and feel free to group in other resources if you have them. If you can't find subs, the job can very quickly become a No Deal. If you are finding subs, then you can begin reaching out to them to gauge if they're interested in quoting the work and attending a site visit if there is one.

It should go without saying, but you are looking for subcontractors to perform the actual statement of work. To really nail the point home, think of building a house. You will more than likely work with a general contractor who is going to see the project through. Does that mean he or she is going to be doing all of the physical labor? Absolutely not. They may not do any of the physical labor.

Their job is to recruit the subcontractors who are actually going to perform the physical labor like mechanical, electrical, plumbing, roofing, and so on. Their job is to also manage timelines, order materials, and oversee the project in its entirety so that all the subs are coordinated and working together nicely. When it comes to working and interfacing with subs, you are like a GC, except in our instance, GC stands for government contractor instead of general contractor.

Google Maps

There are websites and resources on the internet where subcontractor point of contact information is listed for the purposes of reaching out to request a quote. There aren't any sites that I'm personally recommending at this time. I have used a number of them over the years, and they haven't proven to be any more helpful than what's readily available through Google Maps or other map apps that list local business reviews and contact information. For that reason, I recommend you use Google Maps to source local subcontractors for your projects.

You will be able to quickly weed out 2-star service providers and locate 4- and 5-star service providers so that you can dodge any obvious bullets. You will further be able to visit their respective websites and ensure they would be a fit and also be on the lookout for any red flags before you invest anytime into reaching out to them.

Finally, you will also be able to get a geographic reference for how many possible subs are in the area and how far out they are from the site. Some projects are going to be too remote and will be nearly impossible for you to find subs to quote. This will either be an opportunity for you to get creative because there may be low competition (if you can find someone), or it's going to be a No Deal and you save your time and move on.

Intro Call Steps

Once you start making introductory calls to subcontractors, it's helpful to know what you're trying to accomplish and the direction you should be headed in, which is getting a quote. The call doesn't have to be stressful or complicated, but it should accomplish some of the basics that I've laid out.

I don't want to provide you with so much scripting that you're not able to be yourself, so instead, I recommend loosely following the following steps of Open, Educate, Opportunity, Discovery, and Interest, and keep Objecting-Handling and Red Flags in your back pocket for reference when needed.

Open:

"Hello, I have a job local to your area, and I'm wondering who can I speak with to get a quote/estimate?"

Educate:

"We have a government customer that has a need for X, so we are quoting the job for them and are looking for a teaming partner. We read the reviews about your company, and we are interested in possibly working with you on this."

Then share some of the high-level information from the statement of work, like square footage, frequency of service, period of performance, and any upcoming site visit dates to begin to gauge interest.

Opportunity:

"We focus on federal contracting because the contracts often last 2-5 years, so it becomes a form of reliable work without a lot of hassle of trying to get paid, etc. Is that something that appeals to you as well?"

Discovery:

"Has your company ever worked on a government contract as a subcontractor or teaming partner? Do you have a CAGE code or a SAM registration to bid as a Prime?

"What are your typical Payment Terms? The government's payment terms are Net 30, and Net 60 for the first invoice. Do you anticipate any issues with these payment terms? We invoice the government as soon as possible to get the initial ball rolling, and then everything after that is a recurring payment. "

Interest:

"Are you interested in quoting the job? After this call, I will send over a statement of work and site visit terms (if applicable) for you to review."

Objections

You will have to determine whether something is an objection worth trying to overcome or if you're straight up trying to make a horse drink water. You don't want to be in the convincing game because if you successfully do that, it lends to buyer's remorse down the road which is an even bigger waste of your time.

So, instead, think like a recruiter. You put the opportunity in from them, and it's their job to convince you that they are really interested—at least to some degree. If it's you that's doing all of the chasing and them giving you nothing, that is not an objection. They are not truly interested, and you should save your time and move on out of fear of convincing someone who will later have second thoughts about the project.

Objection 1: "I've been burned before."

You may not want to work with this sub if he's going to be once bitten, twice shy. Ask questions to dive deeper into the negative experience. Uncover what happened, and if appropriate, commiserate about how there are bad apples out there that sometimes give contractors a bad name and explain to them how you are different in the necessary ways.

Objection 2: "The government doesn't pay on time."

Ask questions about their experience with this. Why didn't they get paid on time? Let them know that the government does pay on time as long as the work is done properly and invoiced properly. It's often not the government but the prime that causes payment snags and hangups. Decide whether or not this is a red flag to you based on their answer and how unsure they are.

Objection 3: "The government is hard to work for."

Communication is key, and if there were any issues, it's likely because there wasn't strong communication from the start. This will not happen in your contract because you emphasize strong communication with all parties. If the sub is not flexible or trying to change the requirements, then this is a red flag and you should not work with the sub.

Red Flags

A bit clearer than Objections are Red Flags. The Red Flags listed have been time-tested to have a high probability of leading to a nightmare partner on a project. Nothing is worth a nightmare partner, and having no business is better than having bad business.

When interviewing potential subcontractors, always be on the lookout for Red Flags including

- The Teenager
- Boundary Pusher
- My Way or the Highway
- The Nice Guy

Red Flag 1: The Teenager. Has a bad attitude. Acts too busy or distracted and is not serious about working on the project. Has been burned in the past and is very skeptical.

Red Flag 2: Boundary Pusher. Pushes boundaries like not honoring deadlines or providing information as requested.

Red Flag 3: My Way or the Highway. Tries to change the requirement to fit the way they want to do it instead of the way the government is asking for it (particularly after a site visit). This can also take the form of only wanting to perform a certain portion of the contract.

Red Flag 4: The Nice Guy. Says all the right things and almost sounds too good to be true, but when it comes to actually doing anything, he excuses and doesn't deliver.

To summarize, use these scripts as guides to help you in your intro conversations with prospective subs, and to help you navigate the very important decision-making process of finding the right subs for your GovCon Agency, and avoiding the wrong ones.

This act of identifying the right subs is a skill that you will build with repetition.

Overtime, you will evolve your approach to include your style and personality type. Starting with these scripts will not be a silver bullet, but if used properly, they can save you the time of starting from scratch and from potentially costly consequences of ignoring red flags and being stuck with a nightmare teaming partner.

SECTION 4

BIDDING

READING SOLICITATIONS

Everything is going to build from this Reading phase for the government solicitation. This is such an important skill that you need to build. It is truly the "learn to walk before you run" scenario. Without reading and understanding the solicitation, you cannot get estimates from subcontractors because you won't be able to fully inform them of what the job requires.

You won't be able to put together a response that is compliant, let alone one that is competitive enough to be considered for an award. You won't be able to do anything that is accurate or meaningful without having read and understood the solicitation.

The goal of this section is to expose you to a practical approach to reading solicitations along with understanding the most common solicitation sections and government forms so that you can have a bucket for each of these that starts collecting awareness and understanding with every repetition of reading a government solicitation that you perform. With practice and time, this will be a skill that you can master and will even serve as a competitive edge against your competition.

Easter Egg Hunt

The approach that I teach and instill in my clients is that reading a solicitation should be like an easter egg hunt. Meaning, reading a solicitation is an act of finding specific pieces of information. The approach you want to avoid is reading page-by-page, line-by-line, and word-by-word. You will not be effective if that is the approach that you take.

If you have seen my show SAM.gov Bids Live on YouTube, I take you through what seems to be an artistic process to reading government solicitations quickly. For the sake of your understanding, I'm going to make the process much more scientific rather than artistic so that it's now something practical that you can adopt as your own practice.

In order to accomplish this, the best way to go about it seems to provide with you the information and where that information can be found so you can build your skill level and practice getting better at finding it.

SAM.gov Listing Page

The first round of information being mentioned can be found on the SAM.gov List Page, which is the page that opens after you select an opportunity from the SAM.gov search results.

This information includes:

Due Date: Due Date will reflect the date and time proposals are due. Be sure to view Updated Due Date for the most accurate response deadline after any changes.

Set-aside: This reflects which small business program the contract is set-aside for (if any). The most common are Total Small Business, HUBZone, 8(a), ED(WOSB), SD(VOSB), or blank, which indicates an unrestricted or "full and open" solicitation to all bidders.

NAICS Code: A North American Industry Classification System (NAICS) code is selected for every solicitation to reflect which code the government money will be spent under for government tracking purposes. As the bidder, you will want to make sure the NAICS code is added to your SAM.gov entity profile to demonstrate your capabilities to bid under this NAICS code. Also, every code has an associated size standard (dollars or employees). As your business grows, it is possible you outgrow your small business size standard for a specific code, so do your research to familiarize yourself with what these size standards are, and if you think this is something your business is approaching. For quick reference, an average size standard in Professional Services could be $9M - $34M in annual revenue and an average size standard for Construction could be $19M - $40M.

(See images for reference)

ACTIVE

Contract Opportunity

Notice ID
36C24523Q1223

Related Notice

Department/Ind. Agency
VETERANS AFFAIRS, DEPARTMENT OF
Sub-tier
VETERANS AFFAIRS, DEPARTMENT OF
Office
245-NETWORK CONTRACT OFFICE 5 (36C245)

Looking for contract opportunity help?

Procurement Technical Assistance Centers (PTACs) are an official government contracting resource for small businesses. Find your local PTAC for free government expertise related to contract opportunities.

General Information

Contract Opportunity Type: Combined Synopsis/Solicitation (Original)
All Dates/Times are: (UTC-04:00) EASTERN STANDARD TIME, NEW YORK, USA
Original Published Date: Sep 25, 2023 12:19 pm EDT
Original Date Offers Due: Oct 09, 2023 10:00 am EDT
Inactive Policy: Manual
Original Inactive Date: Nov 08, 2023
Initiative:

- None

Classification

Original Set Aside: Total Small Business Set-Aside (FAR 19.5)
Product Service Code: S218 - HOUSEKEEPING- SNOW REMOVAL/SALT
NAICS Code:

- 561730 - Landscaping Services

Place of Performance:
Department of Veterans Affairs Loch Raven VAMC Loch raven , 21218

Attachments: You can gain insight from reading the names attachments are given on the listing page like PWS, PPQ, Pricing Breakdown, Solicitation, Amendment, Drawings, and more. Seeing that these attachments exist immediately shows you what you will have to hunt through to find the specific pieces of information you are looking for.

Attachments/Links

Download All Attachments/Links

Attachments

Document	File Size	Access	Updated Date
1240BE23Q0151 AMEND 0001.pdf	87 KB	Public	Sep 26, 2023
1240BE23Q0151.docx	55 KB	Public	Sep 19, 2023
Attachment 1 Performance Work Statement.docx	41 KB	Public	Sep 19, 2023
Upper Three Creek Map.pdf	6 MB	Public	Sep 19, 2023
Wage Determination.pdf	100 KB	Public	Sep 19, 2023

Contracting: At the bottom of the SAM.gov listing page you will also see the primary and secondary points of contact for contracting. Typically, the primary is the contracting specialist who takes more of an administrative role. The contracting officer is the licensed and warranted officer who is the only one who is able to obligate government funds to the contract. Also, feel free to CC the contracting officer on emails to the specialist.

Contact Information

Contracting Office Address

KO CONTRACTING OFFICE BUILDING 10 PHIPPS RD
PICATINNY ARSENAL , NJ 07806-5000
USA

Primary Point of Contact

Deborah E. Terrell

deborah.e.terrell.civ@army.mil

Secondary Point of Contact

Sharon Wilson-Emmons

sharon.wilson-emmons.civ@army.mil

Solicitation Sections

Here is a brief overview (in order from front to back) of the most common solicitation sections that I believe will be most impactful to your practice. I'm not trying to teach you everything you could know. Rather, I'm trying to give you the most bang for your buck and teach you what you need to know so that you can get started in optimism and continue to skill up from a place of empowerment with reading solicitations.

Practice finding each one of these sections (in order) when reading a solicitation. You may not find them all, but I guarantee you will find some, and you will improve with practice. They may not all be there either, so keep that in mind if you're not finding certain sections.

SF1449/SF1442 Form or Other: The SF1449 is the most common cover sheet (first page) of a solicitation for services contracts. This is the section that you officially print, date, and sign when submitting your offer, and if awarded, will reflect your price along with the contracting officer's signature.

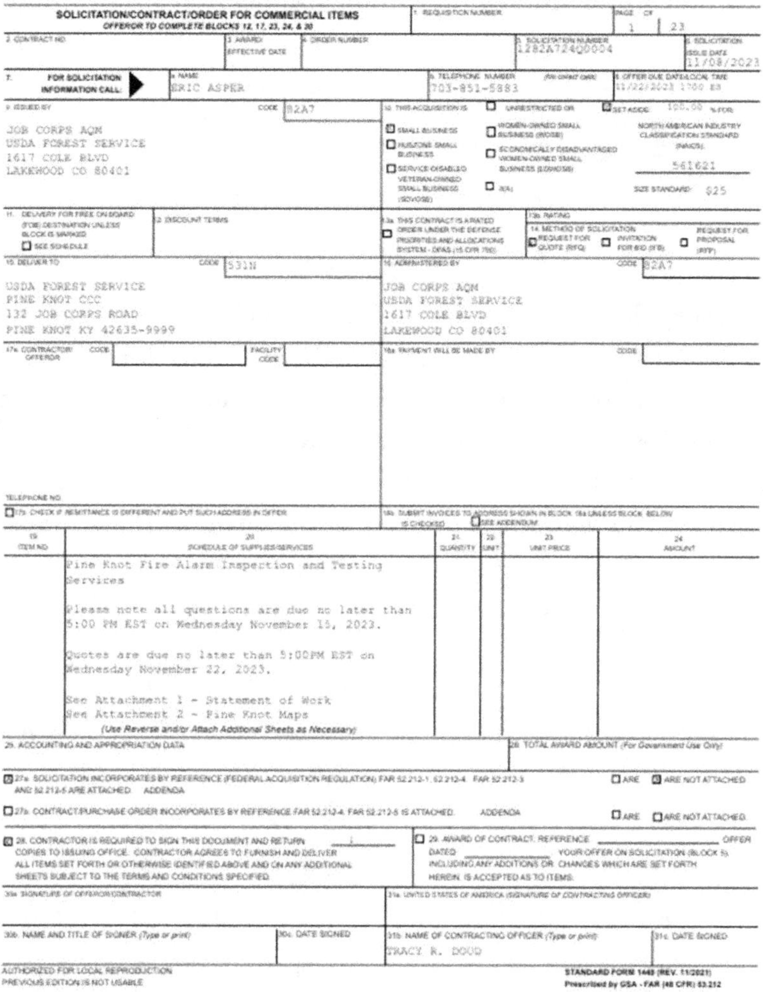

SOLICITATION/CONTRACT/ORDER FOR COMMERCIAL ITEMS
OFFEROR TO COMPLETE BLOCKS 12, 17, 23, 24, & 30

1. REQUISITION NUMBER
PAGE 1 OF 23
2. CONTRACT NO.
3. AWARD/EFFECTIVE DATE
4. ORDER NUMBER
5. SOLICITATION NUMBER 1282A724Q0004
6. SOLICITATION ISSUE DATE 11/08/2023
7. FOR SOLICITATION INFORMATION CALL: a. NAME ERIC ASPER
b. TELEPHONE NUMBER (No collect calls) 703-851-5883
8. OFFER DUE DATE/LOCAL TIME 11/22/2023 1700 ES

9. ISSUED BY CODE 82A7
JOB CORPS AQM
USDA FOREST SERVICE
1617 COLE BLVD
LAKEWOOD CO 80401

10. THIS ACQUISITION IS ☐ UNRESTRICTED OR ☒ SET ASIDE: 100.00 % FOR:
☒ SMALL BUSINESS
☐ HUBZONE SMALL BUSINESS
☐ SERVICE-DISABLED VETERAN-OWNED SMALL BUSINESS (SDVOSB)
☐ WOMEN-OWNED SMALL BUSINESS (WOSB)
☐ ECONOMICALLY DISADVANTAGED WOMEN-OWNED SMALL BUSINESS (EDWOSB)
☐ 8(A)
NORTH AMERICAN INDUSTRY CLASSIFICATION STANDARD (NAICS): 561621
SIZE STANDARD: $25

11. DELIVERY FOR FREE ON BOARD (FOB) DESTINATION UNLESS BLOCK IS MARKED ☐ SEE SCHEDULE
12. DISCOUNT TERMS
13a. THIS CONTRACT IS A RATED ORDER UNDER THE DEFENSE PRIORITIES AND ALLOCATIONS SYSTEM - DPAS (15 CFR 700)
13b. RATING
14. METHOD OF SOLICITATION ☒ REQUEST FOR QUOTE (RFQ) ☐ INVITATION FOR BID (IFB) ☐ REQUEST FOR PROPOSAL (RFP)

15. DELIVER TO CODE 531N
USDA FOREST SERVICE
PINE KNOT CCC
132 JOB CORPS ROAD
PINE KNOT KY 42635-9999

16. ADMINISTERED BY CODE 82A7
JOB CORPS AQM
USDA FOREST SERVICE
1617 COLE BLVD
LAKEWOOD CO 80401

17a. CONTRACTOR/OFFEROR CODE FACILITY CODE
18a. PAYMENT WILL BE MADE BY CODE
TELEPHONE NO.
☐ 17b. CHECK IF REMITTANCE IS DIFFERENT AND PUT SUCH ADDRESS IN OFFER
18b. SUBMIT INVOICES TO ADDRESS SHOWN IN BLOCK 18a UNLESS BLOCK BELOW IS CHECKED ☐ SEE ADDENDUM

19. ITEM NO.	20. SCHEDULE OF SUPPLIES/SERVICES	21. QUANTITY	22. UNIT	23. UNIT PRICE	24. AMOUNT
	Pine Knot Fire Alarm Inspection and Testing Services Please note all questions are due no later than 5:00 PM EST on Wednesday November 15, 2023. Quotes are due no later than 5:00PM EST on Wednesday November 22, 2023. See Attachment 1 - Statement of Work See Attachment 2 - Pine Knot Maps (Use Reverse and/or Attach Additional Sheets as Necessary)				

25. ACCOUNTING AND APPROPRIATION DATA
26. TOTAL AWARD AMOUNT (For Government Use Only)

☒ 27a. SOLICITATION INCORPORATES BY REFERENCE (FEDERAL ACQUISITION REGULATION) FAR 52.212-1, 52.212-4. FAR 52.212-3 AND 52.212-5 ARE ATTACHED. ADDENDA ☐ ARE ☒ ARE NOT ATTACHED.
☐ 27b. CONTRACT/PURCHASE ORDER INCORPORATES BY REFERENCE FAR 52.212-4. FAR 52.212-5 IS ATTACHED. ADDENDA ☐ ARE ☐ ARE NOT ATTACHED.

☒ 28. CONTRACTOR IS REQUIRED TO SIGN THIS DOCUMENT AND RETURN 1 COPIES TO ISSUING OFFICE. CONTRACTOR AGREES TO FURNISH AND DELIVER ALL ITEMS SET FORTH OR OTHERWISE IDENTIFIED ABOVE AND ON ANY ADDITIONAL SHEETS SUBJECT TO THE TERMS AND CONDITIONS SPECIFIED.
☐ 29. AWARD OF CONTRACT: REFERENCE ______ OFFER DATED ______. YOUR OFFER ON SOLICITATION (BLOCK 5), INCLUDING ANY ADDITIONS OR CHANGES WHICH ARE SET FORTH HEREIN, IS ACCEPTED AS TO ITEMS:

30a. SIGNATURE OF OFFEROR/CONTRACTOR
31a. UNITED STATES OF AMERICA (SIGNATURE OF CONTRACTING OFFICER)
30b. NAME AND TITLE OF SIGNER (Type or print)
30c. DATE SIGNED
31b. NAME OF CONTRACTING OFFICER (Type or print) TRACY R. DOUD
31c. DATE SIGNED

AUTHORIZED FOR LOCAL REPRODUCTION
PREVIOUS EDITION IS NOT USABLE
STANDARD FORM 1449 (REV. 11/2021)
Prescribed by GSA - FAR (48 CFR) 53.212

Pricing CLINS: Pricing CLINS are representative of the buckets of money for reaching respective services to be priced separately. This section will inform you of the quantity and unit they are looking for like hours, months, JOB, or something else. This is also one of the areas you can learn if (or how many) option year periods are there.

ITEM NO	SUPPLIES/SERVICES	QUANTITY	UNIT	UNIT PRICE	AMOUNT
0001		10	Months		
	RENTAL OF PORTABLE TOILETS FFP Rental of 6 Portable Toilets IAW the Attached Performance Work Statement (PWS). FOB: Destination MILSTRIP: N0020424RC00BPK PURCHASE REQUEST NUMBER: N0020424RC00BPK PSC CD: W085				
				NET AMT	

Delivery Schedule: Delivery schedule will show you the period of performance, or various periods of performance, for when base and option periods should start and end. It will also include point of contract information and address for the individual who will likely be the COR (contracting officers' representative) on the contract and whom you would communicate with often post-contract award.

DELIVERY INFORMATION

CLIN	DELIVERY DATE	QUANTITY	SHIP TO ADDRESS	DODAAC / CAGE
0001	POP 01-DEC-2023 TO 30-SEP-2024	N/A	N00204 PENSACOLA FL PHILLIP PARKER SEE SCHEDULE PENSACOLA FL 32508 850-452-3198 FOB: Destination	N00204
0002	POP 01-DEC-2023 TO 30-SEP-2024	N/A	(SAME AS PREVIOUS LOCATION) FOB: Destination	N00204
1001	POP 01-OCT-2024 TO 30-SEP-2025	N/A	(SAME AS PREVIOUS LOCATION) FOB: Destination	N00204
1002	POP 01-OCT-2024 TO 30-SEP-2025	N/A	(SAME AS PREVIOUS LOCATION) FOB: Destination	N00204
2001	POP 01-OCT-2025 TO 30-SEP-2026	N/A	(SAME AS PREVIOUS LOCATION) FOB: Destination	N00204
2002	POP 01-OCT-2025 TO 30-SEP-2026	N/A	(SAME AS PREVIOUS LOCATION) FOB: Destination	N00204

Statement of Work (SOW): Universally interchanged with Performance of Work Statement (PWS), the Statement of Work shares the technical details of the work to be performed. This is the most important piece of information for prospective subcontractors to review for this reason. This section may be included in the solicitation document or attached separately as its own document. You will not find much (if any) proposal related information here, but you will find information worth submitting RFIs (Request for Information or "questions") to contracting based off your understanding of what they're requesting here. Always refer to the SOW for job-specific details.

Pikes Peak National Cemetery

Solid Waste and Recycling Removal Contract

Statement of Work

1. Introduction

The National Cemetery Administration is looking for interested parties who wish to submit an offer for the collection and disposal of solid waste and recyclables that are generated on Government owned and Government operated premises at Pikes Peak National Cemetery, Colorado Spring, CO 80925

The specific requirement for recyclables is for the collection and transport to a certified recycling center, of newspaper, magazines, catalogs, phonebooks, office & computer paper, paperboard, cardboard, plastic containers #1 thru #7, metal food and beverage cans, foil wrap and aluminum pans, milk, juice and soup cartons, glass bottles and jars on Government-owned and Government-operated premises at Pikes Peak NC.

The contractor shall provide all management, supervision, labor, tools, materials, supplies equipment and any other items necessary to perform recycling service and solid waste disposal for the National Cemetery. Contractor shall plan, schedule, coordinate and assure effective and economical completion of all contract actions described herein. This contract is for base period with the opportunity of four (4) option years.

2. Requirements

a. Requirement One - General Waste – One (1) SIX Yard Dumpster:
   i. The contractor shall provide one (1) six yard dumpster for the disposal of general waste.
   ii. The contractor shall perform pick-up (empty dumpster) every week (52 pick-ups per year)
   iii. The dumpster shall be located near the cemetery maintenance trailer. The contractor shall contact Pikes Peak personnel to ascertain the proper location for dumpster placement.

b. Requirement Two - Recyclable Waste - One (1), TWO yard Dumpster
   i. The contractor shall provide one (1) two yard dumpster for the disposal of recyclable waste
   ii. The contractor shall perform pick up (empty dumpster) every week (52 pick- ups per year)
   iii. The dumpster shall be located near the cemetery maintenance trailer. The contractor shall contact Pikes Peak personnel to ascertain the proper location for dumpster placement.

c. Requirement Three - General Waste On-Call - One (1) 20 Yard Roll-Off Dumpster (On-Call)
   i. Upon notification of cemetery personnel, the contractor shall deliver, and pickup of one twenty yard roll-off dumpster on an as needed basis. The government estimates that this service will be required 5 times (5 jobs) during each performance period of 12 months.

Wage Determination (WD): The two types of Wage Determination are the Service Contract Act WD (Services) and the Davis Bacon Act WD (construction). They are government by the Department of Labor (DOL). Both are accessible from the homepage of SAM.gov. Each WD will vary based on county.

If a WD applies to your contract, it does not dictate the dollar amount you have to pay your workers. It dictates the minimum amount you have to pay your workers, so that federal contract workers are protected. From it, you will be able to select an "occupation code" associated with a job title and pay rate that "best fits" the labor category you are proposing in your pricing. For services, you will also have to pay health and welfare, vacation, and holidays. For construction, it will include the rate plus the listed fringe benefits.

Area: Arizona County of Pima

Fringe Benefits Required Follow the Occupational Listing

OCCUPATION CODE - TITLE	FOOTNOTE	RATE
01000 - Administrative Support And Clerical Occupations		
01011 - Accounting Clerk I		16.08***
01012 - Accounting Clerk II		18.04
01013 - Accounting Clerk III		20.19
01020 - Administrative Assistant		28.87
01035 - Court Reporter		26.31
01041 - Customer Service Representative I		13.82***
01042 - Customer Service Representative II		15.08***
01043 - Customer Service Representative III		16.94
01051 - Data Entry Operator I		15.54***
01052 - Data Entry Operator II		16.95
01060 - Dispatcher, Motor Vehicle		18.59
01070 - Document Preparation Clerk		16.61
01090 - Duplicating Machine Operator		16.61
01111 - General Clerk I		15.41***
01112 - General Clerk II		16.81
01113 - General Clerk III		18.88
01120 - Housing Referral Assistant		22.55
01141 - Messenger Courier		15.00***
01191 - Order Clerk I		17.75
01192 - Order Clerk II		19.37
01261 - Personnel Assistant (Employment) I		17.65

Federal Regulations: You will see many pages of regulations being incorporated by reference into your solicitations. For example, encouraging a ban on texting when driving for employees. These are Federal Acquisition Regulations (FAR) or commonly Defense Federal Acquisition Regulations (DFAR), and can be referenced through a quick online search or by visiting acquisition.gov or the eCFR.gov (electronic code of federal regulations).

C.2 52.212-5 CONTRACT TERMS AND CONDITIONS REQUIRED TO IMPLEMENT STATUTES OR EXECUTIVE ORDERS—COMMERCIAL PRODUCTS AND COMMERCIAL SERVICES (JUN 2023)

(a) The Contractor shall comply with the following Federal Acquisition Regulation (FAR) clauses, which are incorporated in this contract by reference, to implement provisions of law or Executive orders applicable to acquisitions of commercial products and commercial services:

(1) 52.203-19, Prohibition on Requiring Certain Internal Confidentiality Agreements or Statements (JAN 2017) (section 743 of Division E, Title VII, of the Consolidated and Further Continuing Appropriations Act, 2015 (Pub. L. 113-235) and its successor provisions in subsequent appropriations acts (and as extended in continuing resolutions)).

(2) 52.204–23, Prohibition on Contracting for Hardware, Software, and Services Developed or Provided by Kaspersky Lab and Other Covered Entities (NOV 2021) (Section 1634 of Pub. L. 115–91).

(3) 52.204–25, Prohibition on Contracting for Certain Telecommunications and Video Surveillance Services or Equipment. (NOV 2021) (Section 889(a)(1)(A) of Pub. L. 115–232).

(4) 52.209-10, Prohibition on Contracting with Inverted Domestic Corporations (NOV 2015).

(5) 52.232–40, Providing Accelerated Payments to Small Business Subcontractors (MAR 2023) (31 U.S.C. 3903 and 10 U.S.C. 3801).

(6) 52.233-3, Protest After Award (AUG 1996) (31 U.S.C. 3553).

(7) 52.233-4, Applicable Law for Breach of Contract Claim (OCT 2004) (Public Laws 108-77 and 108-78 (19 U.S.C. 3805 note)).

(b) The Contractor shall comply with the FAR clauses in this paragraph (b) that the Contracting Officer has indicated as being incorporated in this contract by reference to implement provisions of law or Executive orders applicable to acquisitions of commercial products and commercial services:

[] (1) 52.203–6, Restrictions on Subcontractor Sales to the Government (JUN 2020), with Alternate I (NOV 2021) (41 U.S.C. 4704 and 10 U.S.C. 4655).

[] (2) 52.203–13, Contractor Code of Business Ethics and Conduct (NOV 2021) (41 U.S.C. 3509).

[] (3) 52.203–15, Whistleblower Protections under the American Recovery and Reinvestment Act of 2009 (JUN 2010) (Section 1553 of Pub. L. 111-5). (Applies to contracts funded by the American Recovery and Reinvestment Act of 2009.)

Representations and Certifications: These consist of the statements you attest to when completing your SAM.gov entity registration. Often, solicitations will ask you to complete Reps and Certs, but many of you will have already completed them in SAM.gov, so you do not have to fill the entire thing out again. Also, you can download these from your entity profile and save them in a folder for when you are asked to provide them. Visit www.legalmiddleman.com/repsandcerts for a short video on this.

(b) (1) Annual Representations and Certifications. Any changes provided by the Offeror in paragraph (b)(2) of this provision do not automatically change the representations and certifications in SAM.

(2) The offeror has completed the annual representations and certifications electronically in SAM accessed through http://www.sam.gov. After reviewing SAM information, the Offeror verifies by submission of this offer that the representations and certifications currently posted electronically at FAR 52.212-3, Offeror Representations and Certifications--Commercial Products and Commercial Services, have been entered or updated in the last 12 months, are current, accurate, complete, and applicable to this solicitation (including the business size standard(s) applicable to the NAICS code(s) referenced for this solicitation), at the time this offer is submitted and are incorporated in this offer by reference (see FAR 4.1201), except for paragraphs ____

[Offeror to identify the applicable paragraphs at (c) through (v) of this provision that the offeror has completed for the purposes of this solicitation only, if any.

These amended representation(s) and/or certification(s) are also incorporated in this offer and are current, accurate, and complete as of the date of this offer.

Any changes provided by the offeror are applicable to this solicitation only, and do not result in an update to the representations and certifications posted electronically on SAM.]

(c) Offerors must complete the following representations when the resulting contract is for supplies to be delivered or services to be performed in the United States or its outlying areas, or when the contracting officer has applied part 19 in accordance with 19.000(b)(1)(ii). Check all that apply.

(1) Small business concern. The offeror represents as part of its offer that--

(i) It [____] is, [____] is not a small business concern; or

(ii) It [____] is, [____] is not a small business joint venture that complies with the requirements of 13 CFR 121.103(h) and 13 CFR 125.8(a) and (b). [The offeror shall enter the name and unique entity identifier of each party to the joint venture: ____]

Instructions to Offerors: This is the section of the solicitation that lays out what is required in your response, particularly if a response requires a proposal. This will lay out high-level information like font, page limits, and proposal organization. It should also lay out the specifics of what contracting is requesting. For example, what they want in a technical proposal, or the number of past performance projects they want you to provide, etc.

This is often the first place I go when evaluating a prospective Deal because I want to see what is required in my response in order to answer the question, "Do I want to put in the effort to respond to this?"

(viii) 52.212-1 Instructions to Offerors – Commercial Products and Commercial Services (MAR 2023) (Provision)

Addenda to provision 52.212-1:

Addenda to Provision 52.212-1:

For simplified acquisitions, the word quote or quoter is substituted in provision 52.212-1 for the word offer or offeror.

Addenda to Provision 52.212-1 paragraph (b) Submission of Offers:

1) Offerors must have an active entity registration in the System for Award Management in order to submit an offer. https://www.sam.gov/SAM/

2) Offers submitted in response to this solicitation shall include a technical proposal, a price proposal, and contractor representations and certifications.

a) Technical Proposal – The technical proposal shall address the evaluation factors in 52.212-2. At a minimum the technical proposal shall include proof of NFPA certification current and be current with all new NFPA Fire Alarm revisions.

i) Past Performance – provide a list of similar projects completed by your firm over the past three years. Include a brief description of the project, dollar amount, year completed, and project owner contact information (name, phone, and email). The government may use past performance information from any available source. If a

Evaluation Factors: Evaluation factors go hand-in-hand with instructions to offerors. The evaluation factors explain how what contracting is requesting in your proposal will be rated and evaluated. Sometimes these two sections don't line up with each other, and it causes confusion. But if contracting does it properly, these sections should explain how everything that was requested in the instruction to offerors will be evaluated. And if things don't line up, email them the clarifying questions.

(ix) 52.212-2 Evaluation – Commercial Products and Commercial Services (NOV 2021) (Provision)

(a) The Government will award a contract resulting from this solicitation to the responsible offeror whose offer conforming to the solicitation will be most advantageous to the Government, price and other factors considered. The following factors shall be used to evaluate offers:

Technical Evaluation Factors

1. **Past Performance & Relevant Experience**
2. **Key Personnel**
3. **Key Equipment**
4. **Sustainable Acquisition**

Award Determination

The Forest Service's source evaluation will be based on best-value principles. Accordingly, award will be made to the responsible Offeror whose proposal provides the greatest overall value to the Government, price and other factors considered. This best-value determination will be accomplished by comparing the value of the differences in the technical factors for competing offers, based on their strengths, weaknesses, and risks, with differences in their price to the Government. In making this comparison, the Government is more concerned with obtaining superior technical capabilities than with making an award at the lowest overall cost to the Government. However, the Government will not make an award at a significantly higher overall price to achieve slightly superior technical capabilities. As technical scores become closer, price will become more important.

Technical and past performance, when combined, are more important than price.

(b) *Options*. The Government will evaluate offers for award purposes by adding the total price for all options to the total price for the basic requirement. The Government may determine that an offer is unacceptable if the option prices are significantly unbalanced. Evaluation of options shall not obligate the Government to exercise the option(s).

(c) A written notice of award or acceptance of an offer, mailed or otherwise furnished to the successful offeror within the time for acceptance specified in the offer, shall result in a

Also, as part of evaluation factors, we will likely see the procurement method contracting will be using—most notably, either a Best Value evaluation or a Lowest Price Technically Acceptable (LPTA) evaluation. If it's LPTA, you will find that contracting gives you a minimum number of criteria to be what's considered technically acceptable first, and then it will come down to who has the lowest price amongst only the bidders who first meet the minimum requirements.

For a Best Value evaluation, contracting should explain how price factors and non-price factors will be weighted differently, and then your emphasis in your proposal will want to mirror this from what's most important to least important. You may see how your proposal sections will be evaluated using rating labels like unsatisfactory, neutral, satisfactory, good, very good, and excellent.

You may also see confidence ratings like no confidence, neutral confidence, confidence, high confidence, and very high confidence. Of course, everything is important, but you really want to try to do an excellent job with the most heavily weighted areas.

Government Forms

The one rule for government forms is that we don't go looking for them. Many times, I've heard something to the extent of, "Contracting didn't supply an SF1449 form, so I'm on Google trying to find one." If contracting doesn't provide it, you should not be filling it out.

This should be good news because it dramatically limits the possibilities of what you could fill out to only what contracting has provided you with in the solicitation docs. Now, if contracting has asked for it in the instruction to offers, but then hasn't provided it, send them an email and request they add it.

Use this list of common government forms provided to set a precedent for what they may ask of you so that you can start familiarizing yourself with them now.

Common Government Forms

Past Performance Questionnaire (PPQ): PPQs are often a government form included with the solicitation (or attached separately) as a way of requesting information directly from the client. You don't get to fill out your own report card, so PPQs should be sent to the client (subcontractor's clients) ahead of time for them to fill out. Once complete, they should be emailed directly back to contracting. The PPQ will ask a variety of questions specifically about the performance in certain areas/tasks of the project. Make sure clients give you high ratings and that they return it directly to the POC in contracting before the due date.

Pricing Worksheets: We've talked about this in another section already, but these may include supplemental Excel spreadsheets primarily that present the pricing in a broken-down way that contracting wants you to complete. The formulas will already be created and will auto-fill. Be sure that your subs fill this sheet to avoid them giving you pricing in some other way or just as one total number.

Quality Assurance Plans (QASP): This document may be included to show you how your quality will be rated for performance on the project if you win the contract. This is helpful for the sub to know ahead of time to set proper expectations, or it may even affect the approach to the work, depending what's included in the QASP.

Amendments: Amendments are formal public changes to the original solicitation. Amendments may reflect a simple change in due date, or they may reflect changes to the statement of work as a result of new information found at the site visit. Amendments can also be included as a posting of answers to questions asked by industry (bidders). All amendments must be formally acknowledged when you submit your bid by attaching a copy of the pages where you print, sign, and date similar to an SF1449 form cover page.

Q&A: Also known as Requests for Information (RFIs), contractors are allowed to submit questions up to the Q&A deadline that contracting will make note of in the solicitation. These will be posted with an amendment or separately. Never be afraid to submit questions. On the contrary, make it a best practice to increasingly ask intelligent questions about the solicitations you are responding to.

Maps/Drawings: Depending on the type of work, you may see maps and drawings included. These can be used to show terrain, square footage, distance from buildings and parking lots, construction schemas, and architecture plans. This will likely be most useful to whomever you are working with on the project unless you happen to be able to read maps and drawings by trade.

Other: This is not an exhaustive list of forms that you could come up against, but this will definitely get you off to a good start for understanding and trying to find forms on your own. Remember, whenever you have questions, submit those to contracting for further explanation.

Skill Building

Again, reading solicitations is a skill that is built through practice over time, just like anything else. Practice reading solicitations by treating them as an Easter egg hunt to find the SAM.gov listing information, solicitations sections, and government forms that I've laid out for you here. To take it a step further, use the terms I've provided in a ctrl "find" search to try to find them even faster. For example, "Instructions to offerors," "instructions", "evaluation factors," or "evaluation."

Use a terms test to see what quickly comes up for you. I've read through literally thousands of solicitations at this point. So, get started with working your way up to dozens, and then maybe hundreds, and eventually you will be masterful at it.

The last reason why it's so important to practice reading is that every bid is different. This is one of my signature sayings at this point. "Every bid is different." It's hard enough to try to learn something that is like another language. With reading solicitations, the bid requirements are always changing, so it's even harder to learn when it seems like the language keeps changing. It's nuts! And I think it's why you don't see many people signing up for the job to try to teach it.

So, again, this is the approach developed from reading thousands of solicitations, and I'm giving it to you so you don't have to read thousands of solicitations to start quickly building this skill and responding to bids, and winning!

OUTLINE

When it comes to writing proposal responses to government solicitations, the #1 rule is to never start with a blank sheet of paper. For that reason, the Outline phase is a powerful phase that takes you from nothing to something, which very quickly can flip you from being anxious and in overwhelm about getting started writing a proposal to a feeling of "Look Mom, I'm doing it!"

The end goal for the outline should really be to set yourself up in the Proposal Writing phase to be able to plug-and-chug a lot of your proposal. You are probably brand new at this, so it won't be a lot of plugging and chugging at first, but you will find after responding to a few solicitations, you will begin to build a library of your own proposal content for your company that you will be able to reuse and customize for future solicitation responses.

It will be a bit more work getting started when you have nothing, and that's why I provide all of my clients with pre-written templates and fully customizable proposal content so they can start that much faster. You don't need to have it, and I will share some helpful starting points here to continue to empower you in the area of proposal writing no matter what your starting point is.

Skeleton

There is no such thing as a copy-and-paste proposal template. Every bid is different, so I'm providing a skeleton that you will be able to use flexibly to match the requirements of your proposal so that you are compliant.

In order to complete this flexible skeleton, you will be utilizing what you've learned in the Reading phase of your response. You need to be able to find the information to apply the skeleton correctly. Use what you've learned in the Reading phase to help you knock this skeleton out of the park!

Let's discuss briefly each of **the areas of your flex-skeleton:**

Page Format

Traditional acceptable font for government solicitations is 12-point size with Times New Roman font. I've occasionally seen them request differently, so be sure to be looking for different font requests (like Calibri). This, however, is a good standard formatting to apply to your templates as you create them.

Widely acceptable formatting for pages will include page numbers, solicitation numbers, and your company name between the headers and footers. Compared to the font/text, there is a bit more fluidity with page formatting. We see contracting officers requesting more, less, or different information than this. Use this as a default, and then read your solicitation to learn if contracting has a preference different than this.

In addition, it's very important to understand if contracting wants all sections of your proposal in one document or as separate documents. Also, do they want them named specifically as certain volumes? These can serve as tripwires, whereas, if you don't follow these exact formatting instructions, your proposal can technically be thrown out before it's even reviewed.

We often see contracting asking for sections to be broken out as Volume I, Volume II, and Volume III, with specific naming conventions for each. Similarly, when there are price factors and non-price factors, contracting will need those split into entirely different documents so that each proposal section can be evaluated individually and without other influences or bias. Sometimes, they will even request not to put the company name on the proposal section pages for that same reason.

It can feel like a lot of nit-picking, but in the eyes of contracting, they can be reviewing dozens and dozens of responses. In order to make a fair and reasonable determination, they need everything to be lined up apple-to-apple. If something isn't lining up with what was asked, it's getting thrown out right from the beginning.

For all these reasons, use these as acceptable guidelines, and then properly read your solicitation to find the exact details of the format that contracting is requesting. If they don't state anything, and you're feeling uneasy about the lack of direction, feel free to email contracting within the Q&A period with your planned formatting and get feedback as to what would be acceptable.

Cover Page

Cover pages are always recommended, but as you'll hear me say a lot in this area, always check to see what contracting is asking for. A standard proposal cover page will have the company name, solicitation number, project title, and date in the center. On the lower left or right half, we put the address information for contracting, including the name of whom the proposal is being sent, their physical contracting address, and any other POC information. The point of contact information can be found at the bottom of the SAM.gov listing page for the solicitation where they list contracting's email address.

Are you starting to see how every bid is different now?

Government Profile

Not everyone uses this and it's not something I see specifically asked for. Consider a government profile as an option based on how you personally feel about it as part of your library of content. A government profile houses of all your government contracting information in one easy-to-access spot near the introduction of your proposal.

The profile should consist of your Unique Entity ID, your CAGE code, your commonly used NAICS codes (adjusted to match each solicitation), and any set-asides your company has including 8(a), HUBZone, EDWOSB, SD(VOSB), and Total Small Business. You may also include your company website or a link to a downloadable version of your company's capability statement.

Again, this profile is optional, but it can make it easy for contracting to access everything they need about your company all in one place. And since not everyone does it, you could make a small case for you standing out. I would not include this if you're trying to come under a tight page limit or if you see contracting being very strict about the proposal information to be provided.

Table of Contents (TOC)

Table of contents is generally not necessary for RFQ responses and other responses that have a very low page count and primarily focus on the price only. As you get into more lengthy and in-depth RFP responses, it will become more necessary to reflect your proposal organization in the Table of Contents. The good news for you is that if you follow this outlining phase properly, your skeleton outline will be a perfect mirror for the information that should be captured in your table of contents. And if you include a TOC built in as part of your outline, it will be exactly that.

Using Microsoft Word, you can easily create an effective TOC by selecting References > Table of Contents > Automatic table, and then apply the heading styles to the titles of each section that you want to show up in your table of contents. The TOC will automatically apply and update dynamically with appropriate page number references as you build out your outline.

Technical

A technical section of your response may or may not be required. If it's a price-only solicitation, or price and past performance only, you will not be required to provide a technical response. For this outline, we are defaulting both technical and past performance as part of the format because it's what you will be encountering over various bids, so you will have it when you need it. For the instances when it's not required, simply do not include the respective section.

Generally, a technical section answers the question, "How will the work be completed?." This is not a listing of *what* you would do, but rather *how* you would do it. Contracting stresses to not merely parrot back what is requested in the Statement of Work. They want an explanation of what your (and your sub's) approach is going to be.

Imagine if you were vetting contractors to replace the roof on your home. You wouldn't only look at the price. You would want to know what is different about the roofing approach that different companies are using. Also, is it going to void any warranties or gold fortification standards? What are they going to do if it rains? How long will it take? What type of shingles? How long will it take? These questions can go on and on.

Much of the time, contracting is going to give you clear direction about what they want in a technical response including factors and subfactors, etc. Regardless, understand that this is the spirit that you should be going into a technical response with. And when contracting does ask for a technical response but doesn't tell you what they want (this will happen), then you have this as guidance to not parrot back the SOW. Instead, explain your approach to the work the same way you would want someone who is putting a new roof on your home to explain their approach to you.

Past Performance

Past performance may be requested as an additional evaluation factor to showcase work you've done previously. If you follow the Legal Middleman Method, you probably don't have any past performance. We've spoken about this already, but have no fear, the subcontractor's past performance is here.

First, as always, provide past performance project examples to contracting in accordance with any specific direction they have provided. When you think past performance, think of the 2 R's. Relevancy and Recency. Relevancy means how similar the scope of the project being cited is to the project that is being quoted. In other words, don't use drop-shipping equipment past performance on a janitorial bid. Recency means how long ago the work was performed, and you want to keep it in the 3–5-year window.

When requesting past performance from subcontractors, you can request based on the information below, and then plug the information you receive into your proposal. It's also at this time that you can start thinking about using "Teaming" language.

For example, to tee up your past performance, you can include an opening statement,

"ABC, LLC and its Teaming Partner XYZ, LLC present the following past relevant projects completed in recent years."

Project Title:

Period of Performance:

Place of Performance:

Magnitude:

Brief Scope:

References (optional):

Contracting will usually request up to 3 project examples to satisfy past performance, so as a standard, you can request 3 projects from your subcontractor with this information to be provided for each, unless contracting indicates differently.

Price

I have a standard Word.doc table that I use as a pricing placeholder for part of the outline. I may need it or I may not. If I do, it saves time because it's already templated with default pricing CLINS where all I would have to do is add in the CLIN info from the solicitation. If contracting is asking to only fill the price on a separate form or as a different volume, then I will either delete or extract the table from the outline as needed.

When your numbers come in, it's helpful and mentally calming during crunch mode to have somewhere to house pricing information—even if you will have to separate or format it differently prior to submission. I recommend creating something similar that you can use as a go-to placeholder when you start to get numbers in from quotes.

In summary, consider using these areas or something close to them to build your flexible skeleton that you can approach solicitations with. It will automatically give you confidence, and you will never have to start with a blank sheet of paper. Immediately add, edit, and delete from the skeleton to match what is actually required in your response, and you will be well on your way to teeing up a compliant proposal response in a future phase.

PRICING

Let's go ahead and talk in totality about the pricing phase. I'm going to touch on three aspects of pricing: Government Pricing, Competitor's Pricing, and Company Pricing.

For Government Pricing, we're going to review Wage Determinations and Pricing CLINS. At this point, we have already hit on both, so we're creating this section to be a reference with all the pricing information in one place.

We're also going to be hitting on your competitor's pricing. I'm going to show you some places to review and research, and then we're going to talk just a bit about your company pricing to tie everything together that we're touching on.

This particular training is meant to be a resource for you. It's not meant to be a step-by-step approach. Come back and use this often and refer to it as you need it, and then be sure to ask questions to contracting as you're working on actual bids.

We will get started with the first section of Pricing, which is Government Pricing.

Government Pricing

Wage Determinations:

Let's further review wage determinations to get started. According to the definition on Sam.gov, "A wage termination is a set of wages, fringe benefits, and work rules that the U.S. Department of Labor, the DOL, has ruled to be prevailing for a given labor category and a given locality"[9].

Or in other words, as I would say, it reflects the minimum amount of what you must pay your people. So, when you're seeing a wage determination with Service Contract Act or Davis-Bacon Act—professional services or construction respectively—then just know that's what it's trying to tell you.

If you want to take a glance at these, you can go over to sam.gov and they have a wage determinations option to select. The way this works is they're based on occupation code. For the professional services side of things, it's also based on the title. What you do with the wage determination is choose the best title or code that fits your category. What's interesting when it comes to WDs is that many times you don't find what is an exact match.

So, what you have to do is match up what is going to be the closest fit to what you're offering. Keep in mind that the whole purpose for you as an employer is to protect yourself in case an employee contacts the Department of Labor and claims that they're not getting paid enough or that they're not getting enough benefits. This is to protect federal contract workers.

And if the DOL hears that and they come and knock on your door, you want to have something to demonstrate that you are meeting the minimum requirements. Now, if you're choosing something that doesn't fit from the list, then that doesn't make sense, and the DOL is probably going to correct you. If you are meeting your minimums, then there's nothing to worry about.

When it comes to construction, a rate and fringe amount is listed on the WD. You have to pay both. It's not one or the other. Some companies get in trouble for thinking since they offer insurance and they meet the pay rate so they don't have to pay fringe. No, you have to pay them the rate and the fringe.

For construction, the fringe is actually made up of other things like health and welfare, vacation time, and paid holidays. That all adds up to be fringe benefits. Federal contract workers are entitled to this. You can find these definitions, as described, in the wage determination itself.

Pricing CLINS:

These are the buckets of money that you are going to become very familiar with as you start bidding. We have covered a lot of this already, so I just want to introduce some of the naming conventions to help get you more familiar with the application of Pricing CLINS and the terminology.

For units, you may recognize these abbreviations. This is what they stand for:

"MO" = Months (duration)

"EA" = Each (quantity).

"JOB" = One Job (project)

"FTE" = Full-time Equivalent (staffing)

"Hour" = One Hour

"Base Year" = always the first year of a contract

"Option Years" = always future years (Option years are not guaranteed, so do a good job.)

The government may default a unit or a quantity, and that just means they're telling you how much of what they want. For example, a default of 1920/2080 hours is indicative of 1 full-time person working for a year.

Typically, the more Pricing CLINS the better because it means the pricing is broken down further. You will be able to see more clearly what you are pricing, as opposed to having one Pricing CLIN with everything compiled in there. It also makes the quotes you're getting from your subs easier to compare on a line-by-line basis to see where they differ. Also, when you're invoicing, you are essentially billing out against these individual buckets of money. So, you'll see this reflected in your invoices to the government as well.

USASpending.gov[10]:

In USA Spending, you can see which government agencies are buying the most of your NAICS codes and how much they're spending. So, although it doesn't influence your pricing directly, this is an interesting search I want you to be able to run that may influence your NAICS code decisions, as well as empower you to better understand where the government is spending its money.

This is a very simple but powerful search. At USA Spending, if you select "Search Award Data", you will have many filters to toggle through. We will use "All Years" and "NAICS code" for this search. After you complete these 2 fields and submit a search, the table will update. Select the "Categories" option all the way to the right and you will be presented with a hierarchical bar graph of agencies that spend the most to the least of this particular NAICS code.

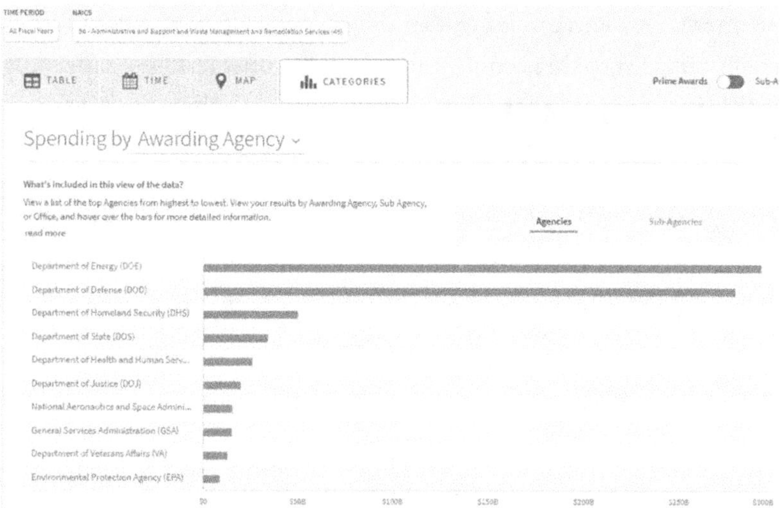

When I first found this, I couldn't believe my eyes, and I wanted to show everyone. You can also select sub-agencies to see the breakdown of the DoD, for example, so you can also see how much individually the Army, Air Force, and Navy buys, and more. So, I hope you enjoy it!

Competitor Pricing

Now, let's talk about some of the factors that play into your competitor's pricing and what it means to you.

Request for Information:

An incumbent is a company that's already doing the work, so if there is one, we can submit an RFI to contracting to request that information. Imagine that. The question becomes what the price of the incumbent's contract is.

This becomes one of your questions for the Q&A with the government. When you make a deal/no deal, one of the first things that you want to do is communicate with contracting—especially if this is an ongoing service contract—and ask them if there is an incumbent providing this level of effort (LOE).

And if there is an incumbent, as if the government can please provide the recent contract award number and contract award value. That way you can get that basic information to work with. It's going to help you a lot with your pricing.

But there is one caveat.

For example, take an existing landscaping contract and say they're adding a territory or removing a territory on the upcoming contract. If you were to price based on the old scope/contract value alone, you would be pricing incorrectly. Since you're not able to obtain old solicitation documents without requesting a FOIA (Freedom of Information Act), you could end up being way off if contracting modified the scope. So, this becomes a good jumping-off spot, but not necessarily an exact value.

Another empowering question to ask contracting if you feel this could be your situation is what scope changes have been made from the old contract to the new contract. This will help to buffer the deviations caused by any modifications to the scope.

FPDS.gov[11]:

If you do get the award number and it's different from the old solicitation number, you can type it into fpds.gov. Just type it in the search, and it's going to pull up details on the contract. You can click "view," and it'll show you the action obligation, the point of contact in contracting, the number of offers received, and the set-aside.

You will be able to see how much funding has been used from the contract. Altogether, it's a lot of interesting information that you would probably want to know if you're putting a response together. This is really a go-to activity and something that a lot of large and established contract organizations use as a standard business procedure as part of their capture management processes.

This becomes something you very much want to start practicing regularly, too. When you are bidding on contracts, if you can't get close in your pricing, you're going to lose a lot of your bids. So, we want to get as close as possible, which means being as informed as possible and using all the resources we have at our disposal.

GSA eLibrary[12]:

There's also a resource called the GSA eLibrary. Many of us have heard of GSA schedules, right? But many of us are not on a GSA schedule. Getting on a GSA schedule can cost you $20,000-$30,000. It's also going to cost you a year of your time. You're going to need audited accounting systems, and you're going to have to put together pricing tier lists and pricing catalogs to essentially show and market to the government what your prices are for certain things.

The good news for us is all the information resulting from that process from other companies (like our competitors) getting approved is made available to us publicly for free. And it's broken down into categories so we can search for what's nearest our offer.

If you go over to GSA eLibrary, you can just type that into Google, it'll pull right up. Depending on which of these you're interested in researching, you can look through categories like IT, Facilities, Professional Services, and more. Select what you're interested in. There's going to be one or two questions to help you drill down, so I didn't include those. Use your best guess and play around with it.

You will arrive at a page, A through Z of the companies in this area, and they'll have all of these price lists and catalogs, and as you open them, it'll show you labor categories and price escalations for those categories. It also gives you descriptions for these categories that have to be defined and accepted to get on the GSA schedule as well.

All of this work is put together in these downloadable documents that are available free to us to do our research. If you're one who enjoys doing this level of research, this is a tremendous resource that you can start using.

Company Pricing

When it comes to Company Pricing, there's not a whole lot additional that I want to say because your pricing is really going to be based on working with the subs. But I just want to give you a few more tips for your company's pricing.

Pricing Tips

#1. Don't price so low you can't sleep at night. There is such a thing as bad business, and you don't want it. Bad business can become so bad that it prevents you from bidding on other contracts. They can terminate your contract for cause, and they can give you a black eye on your report card that can sway future agencies away from working with you. You don't want to go so low that you cut things too close or underbid the contract and find yourself at this level of risk. It's not worth it.

#2. Price for the evaluation factors. We're continuing to touch on the two commonly known evaluation factors. They are Lowest Price Technically Acceptable (LPTA) and Best Value. So again, the lowest price is going to be if you check the boxes and you meet the technical minimums. Then they're going to move you to round two in the selection.

In round two, whoever made it this far with the lowest price is going to be the winner. Again, you have to meet the minimum requirements first. If you don't check this box, they throw you out. They don't even look at your price, even if you are the lowest. That's how the lowest price works.

For Best Value, the government's willing to pay more to get more and to have a higher level of confidence in the service you're going to be providing. That confidence will be demonstrated through your proposal including your technical, your past performance, and your price reasonableness.

#3. The government does not have deep pockets. Educate the subcontractors to formulate their pricing like they would in the commercial space. A lot of subcontractors hear "government," and immediately think "deep pockets." Incorrect.

Margins and competition are very comparable to the commercial space. Your teaming partner could literally be going up against their commercial competitors on a government bid, so they should be pricing accordingly. Subcontractors lose more bids for prime government contractors than anything else, and it's for that reason that the primes need to educate the subcontractors on how to bid competitively.

To drive this point home, on larger contracts, contracting will even ask you to submit cost and pricing data reflective of the market prices in order to justify your prices. So, it doesn't hurt to start making this part of your company's pricing process now.

#4. It is a numbers game. You will lose many more contracts than you will win. If you are new, it's going to take you time and a lot of losing to figure out the correct pricing strategy for the Deals you are going after for your GovCon Agency. Don't lose patience or get down on yourself when you don't win. Focus on improving and getting better with each and every submission. Eventually, you will get better, and when you get better, you start winning.

If you are trying something for 6-12 months and you're still stuck in the same exact spot, you have to switch something up. Again, it's called the Number's Game, but that doesn't mean don't learn from your mistakes. If you're not learning and you're continuing to do the same things wrong, it's no longer a numbers game. It becomes a game of futility.

PROPOSAL WRITING

During the Proposal Writing phase, you are bringing everything together. Those who are inexperienced could think proposal writing is just sitting behind a computer typing away. Proposal Writing is a lot more than that. It's a lot of coordination, communication, and organization. It's research. It's going back and rereading sections for the tenth time.

And it feels like quite a messy process. *This* is the process. *This* is what it is supposed to feel like if you're doing it right.

It's important to note at this stage, you should have at least 2 potential teaming partners provide their pricing/proposal response for the job. You, of course, will not be including both (or all) of them in your final proposal that you submit to the government.

You will want to lead with the strongest teaming partner. You will want to select the price/proposal that best aligns with the procurement strategy for the solicitation so that the proposed team stands the best chance of winning. This is the time when you are essentially choosing the sub you want to work with and including their information in your response.

In the spirit of coordinating all of this, I'm going to touch on the different areas you will be coordinating with your teaming partner during the Proposal Writing phase, including the Proposal Outline, Technical Sections, Past Performance, Pricing, Government Forms, and Document Management.

Proposal Outline

If you followed the outline phase properly, you should have teed yourself up quite nicely for proposal writing. If you haven't already, you will want to customize everything from your outline to match the solicitation requirements. This includes your cover page and cover letter, updating your Table of Contents, making a decision about including a government profile, and laying out only the necessary sections from the list of possibilities including a Technical section, Past Performance section, and a Pricing section, as we've previously covered.

Depending on how much content you have already written (if any), you can start to pull from your company library to start to plug-and-chug the sections of your outline. This also includes the information you receive from your subcontractors/teaming partners. As you retrieve from your library and receive from your extended team, you can start to plug in the pieces to the sections of your outline, and slowly but surely, it will start to come together.

Technical Sections

Technical sections may include, but are not limited to resumes, staffing plans, quality control plans, project management plans, timelines, credentials, and responding to how you will meet the requirements of the statement of work. If some mix of this is required for your proposal response, you will be coordinating with your teaming partner to provide the best information to include in your response. When it comes to the managerial-type plans and responses, you will want to develop this as part of your content library, so you can explain in future solicitations what your tailored approach will be for each respective project.

Past Performance

If you don't have any projects yet that are relevant, you will be utilizing your teaming partner's past performance. As previously discussed, the default is 3 projects over the last 5 years that are recent and relevant. Also, don't forget to provide proper instructions for Past Performance Questionnaires for your partner if they are being submitted. As you win contracts as a legal middleman, you will be building your own past performance as a prime contractor, and you will be able to use that to directly satisfy past performance requirements on future solicitations where the scope of work is similar (relevant).

Pricing

At this phase, you're also starting to finalize pricing. Hopefully, you are in the process of having quotes sent to you or maybe you've already received them. Now, you want to begin adding your costs and markups to the quotes so that you have finalized the numbers.

Once you have this, you will be ready to add the finalized pricing to whatever pricing format has been requested, including Excel pricing breakdown sheets, Pricing CLINS, pricing tables, or something else provided by the government. Again, if you do not have a proper pricing format that is provided to you, you may email contracting your plan for presenting the pricing, and request direction be given if your intended approach will suffice.

Government Forms

Do you remember the rule for government forms? We do not go hunting for government forms, we complete what is provided to us. If something is requested but not provided, then we email contracting and ask them to provide it.

Amongst the government forms you could come across, we've discussed SF1449/1442 forms, PPQs, Reps and Certs, Amendments, and Pricing Worksheets. This list is not exhaustive but greatly prepares you for what you will come across.

Be sure to organize the forms in your response in any particular sequence that contracting has provided. Also, you can attach forms separately from your response (if allowed) as part of the body of your email submission to provide a cleaner proposal response. Always reference separately attached forms in your proposal so that contracting knows they have been included separately.

Government forms are ever-changing and evolving. Be sure to ask for guidance from contracting about anything that you don't understand. I can't stress this enough. Changes to forms, mistakes from contracting, and interpretations of small details can all result in different outcomes for the final contract award. So, be confident, and don't be afraid to ask for more direction when you don't understand something. You likely aren't the only one.

Document Management

Having effective document management software is going to be something you want to invest in sooner rather than later. Many people use Adobe Acrobat to modify, edit, or extract PDF documents. I like the software called Smallpdf[13]. I am not an affiliate of theirs. It's just a very intuitive and easy-to-use software. It's cheaper than Adobe, and I like the visual layout they provide of the documents you are working on.

At a minimum, you're going to need to be able to sign and input pricing onto PDF forms, so you need to make sure you have the software capabilities to meet these minimum tasks. Once you find yourself needing to extract pages or add government forms to a certain volume of a proposal, you will want to have software that makes this easy. Proposal writing can be hectic enough. You don't want software adding more stress to the mix. Let software make things easier for you.

Words to the Wise

#1. Be very conservative in providing something in your proposal that the government has not requested. If it doesn't clearly fit into a section that's being rated, it will just be in the way, and it also makes it harder to find what the government is trying to find. We call this fluff. Keep fluff to a very low minimum. Fluff usually finds its way into a proposal because it's something the writer wants to include, rather than it being something the reader wants to read. This becomes increasingly important with the increased governing of the proposal response. Hence, my thoughts on including a government profile depends on the bid.

#2. Keep colors, illustrations, graphs, and charts to a minimum. Unless otherwise requested, these also walk the fence on being fluff. Contracting has to print these out for the evaluation and source selection process. The more copies they have to print, the more problems at scale your colors and visual demonstrations become.

#3. Proposal layout and organization continue to be underrated. Way more significant than the bells and whistles of colors and charts, is the clear layout and organization of your proposal. In accordance with the instructions to offerors or whatever you've been asked to provide to be evaluated, how easy do you make it for contracting to find the information they are looking for? And how clearly do you lay that information out for them to review?

This is huge. I can metaphysically feel contracting officers' heads nodding as I write this. When it comes to small business contracting, if you can get exceptional at spoon-feeding contracting exactly what they're asking for and make your response extremely clear and obvious for them, then you're going to move to the top 10-20% of offers received. *Just by doing this.*

Why? Because most other contractors are really bad at it. They didn't read this book. Or they only do it partly for their proposal response, but then they're missing something else. Match the requirement in sequence, take out the fluff, and do a good job of answering contracting's questions, and you will move to the front of the line.

#4. As a carry-on from the last point, avoid being eliminated by trip wires. If contracting asks for a specific font type/size, then give it to them. Don't exceed page limitations for sections. Name sections and volumes in accordance with what they tell you to name them (if anything). Don't miss your deadlines/times for site visits, questions, and proposal submissions. Do not parrot back the statement of work as bullet points saying what your company will do. Instead, explain HOW you will do it. And don't submit unbalanced or unreasonable pricing as part of your proposal response.

REVIEW, SUBMIT, DEBRIEF

The final phase is the Submit phase. I call this phase the submit phase, but it's made up of a few steps that all relate to submitting your offer to the government. These steps include Review, Submission, and Debrief, and I will expand on each of these more. Keep in mind that the goal is to have a process for submitting compliant and competitive offers, and so you can use this as a system that scales over time.

Review

The term Red Team review is used a lot in the government contracting space, and consists of team review and delegation. For some larger GovCons, it's appropriate, but if you're a brand new GovCon Agency as a team of 1,2, or 3, a full-blown Red Team Review is not going to be possible or necessary. I have 2 recommendations instead that would be appropriate for you to get started reviewing your offers prior to submission.

The first recommendation is to use a simple compliance matrix to review your proposal response for compliance. Don't know what this is? It's very simple. At its core, a compliance matrix reflects each of the requirements of solicitation from the instructions to offerors/evaluation factors or in whatever way contracting presented it to you as an individual item.

Then, for each item you cite where in your proposal you responded to that item. If you want to take it a step further, you can also include a self-rating on how well you think you satisfied the response to each item. This ensures you didn't overlook anything.

My second recommendation is to give the compliance matrix to someone else to review your proposal. We all have blind spots, so what someone else with fresh eyes could easily catch becomes a low-hanging fruit activity for something that we wouldn't catch after hours of review on our own. If you don't use the compliance matrix, you can give your proposal to them for review, but unless they are educated on govcon proposals, it's not going to be really effective for you.

When all is finished, run the spell and grammar check and triple-check your pricing numbers. Make sure there are no decimal points or commas out of place. Also, make sure the right numbers are being used for the right line items or pricing CLINS. Finally, ensure all the files, volumes, and proposal sections, all follow the naming conventions that contracting has instructed (if any).

Submission

When you submit your offer to contracting, you want to make sure you have everything set up. Have all of your attachments in the email draft ready to go. The submission email response can be short.

Here is an example:

To: Michael.rece@gsa.gov

Subject: 47PE0321R0001/ ABC, LLC Response

Hello Michael,

ABC, LLC offers its response to Solicitation 47PE0321R0001 to provide renovation to the Clyde Atkins US Courthouse in Miami, FL.

Our response includes our Technical Proposal (with bid bond), Pricing Proposal, and completed Reps and Certs.

Please let me know if you have any questions, and we look forward to an opportunity to provide the subject services to the GSA.

Please confirm receipt of this submission email and its attachments.

Respectfully,
Your Name

Make a note to always ask for confirmation of receipt in your submission email. If they didn't get it, you're the one who's going to be hurting, and technological things do happen. If I haven't received confirmation within a couple of hours, I pick up the phone and call the contracting officer to request receipt. Sometimes, they will check their email with you on the phone and they will verify your company name and confirm they received it.

After receipt is confirmed, time will start to go by. You will start to get antsy and wonder if it's been awarded to someone else yet because you haven't heard anything it could've been. They could also still be in deliberations. Contracting could also be on vacation. There's a lot that could potentially be going on.

If there isn't obvious reason for a contract to take many months (6-12) to be awarded, I recommend 2-4 weeks as an appropriate window to follow up with contracting to see if they have an anticipated award timeframe.

See example below:

Follow-Up

To: michael.rece@gsa.gov

Subject: 47PE0321R0001/ ABC, LLC Response

Hello Michael,

My company responded to Solicitation 47PE0321R0001 on XX/XX. I wanted to follow up to see if an award was made, or if there is an anticipated award date.

Please don't hesitate to reach out if there are any questions with our response that I can help clarify.

Respectfully,
Your Name

Debrief

A proposal debrief is where you are able to gain feedback from the contracting officer on the proposal you submitted. What did you do well on and what did you not do well on? If you get them on the phone, sometimes they will really open up and tell you a lot. This is invaluable feedback for your growth in the space.

Debriefs shall be requested in writing to the contracting officer within 72 hours of an award being made. Once you find that there's an award made, request a debrief. Even if you win, request a debrief because there is always something to improve on, and it also helps to build your confidence when contracting validates something that you did very well. This way you know to use what you did very well on for future proposals.

Proposal debriefs are reserved for proposals resulting from an RFP. If the bid was a price-only quotation (RFQ), there's not really much feedback they can give you. They will sometimes tell you where you fell in the pecking order, but they won't tell you what the other company's prices were. Contracting may even decline the request for debrief for this same reason.

To request a debrief, feel free to use the simple example below:

Debrief Request

To: dayna.canu@navy.mil

Subject: SPMYM421Q0016/ Debrief Request

Hello Dayna,

ABC, LLC requests a proposal debrief for our response to Solicitation SPMYM421Q0016.

Please let me know if we can coordinate this to receive feedback on our solicitation response submission.

Respectfully,
Derek James

In summary, I highly recommend you use the Review, Submit, Debrief process as a staple in your proposal submission practice. Use the email templates as starter templates so that you know "what right looks like" when you start submitting offers. I also have the list of acceptable questions to ask in a proposal debrief available at my website www.legalmiddleman.com/debrief[14].

SECTION 5

AWARD

AWARD, WHAT'S NEXT?

You've received an award or you maybe got a verbal that you're about to receive an award. Here are some of the immediate next steps I recommend that you take. You can also review this section to prepare for a future award so that you know what to expect when it happens.

Step 1.

The first thing to do when you win an award—especially if you're legal middlemanning—is to communicate and possibly negotiate with your teaming partner. Notify the sub that you won and that you would be moving forward, and you want to make sure that they are still good to move forward with the project, too. If you don't have a partner, then that's going to make it really hard for you to fulfill the contract.

Now, you don't have to do this, everything is a negotiation. You can offer the sub an opportunity to come down on their price. You can more easily do this because now you have an award, and that means more bargaining power. You can give them an opportunity to come down 5% or more, whatever seems fair, and then you can move forward with them if they agree.

Like I said, it's up to you if you want to do this. You don't ever want to make the sub feel like they've already given you their best price and now you're twisting their arm too much. This is why it's a negotiation. Subs do put padding in their pricing because they know that it's a negotiation too, so many are already prepared to come down at the end. And if you skip it, then you could just be leaving money on the table.

Treat this on a situation-by-situation basis, but it is something to consider. The goal is to select the best sub as your teaming partner early on. When you do that, you're going to sign a teaming agreement with them as well. There are templates for this you can find online. I also offer templates for this included in the library of templates I offer as part of my programs. You will want to customize this to your contract and get your teaming partner locked in so you can move to the next step.

Step 2.

If you are using funding to finance the deal, you want to make sure that you have funding in place. That means, if you're using a factoring company or another finance company, you want to ensure your terms with them to make sure you will be able to finance the project.

If you're just relying on a net 30-day billing cycle with the government, and then you're going to release payment to the subs as a reimbursement, that's fine. You can do that with service contracts. If you don't need financing support, you can skip to the next step.

But if you are using some sort of financing, again to float, perhaps you have to buy a material. Or it's a contract that pays based on milestone payments rather than net 30, so you may need the capital. You just want to make sure you have this locked in with your finance provider at this early stage before moving forward with an award.

Step 3.

In Step 3, you can review and sign the award. When reviewing, you want to make sure contracting puts the exact numbers in the Pricing CLINS. When contracting types in the dollar amounts, sometimes they miss a comma, or they miss a decimal point, or they miss a number. You need to make sure that when they send you the award, the price, and all the CLINS are accurate. You want to add up any of the broken-down amounts and make sure they also add to the total amount.

You also want to review the scope to make sure there are no changes to the statement of work. In addition, you're really browsing over the entire contract, checking for any highlights, and checking for anything that may have been added in differently from what you submitted. It's not that the government is necessarily doing something malicious, but things can happen—especially when multiple people are involved—so I just want you to protect yourself in this way.

Now, if there are questions or clarifications, this is essentially your last chance at this stage before signing and returning to push those back to contracting. It's not a good time for last-minute questions, but if there was something that was discovered last minute, you can communicate that before starting the work. There's no good time for that sort of thing, but sooner is always better.

If everything is good on the award, sign and return the form that they've issued to you. You may not have to sign it, it may be a unilateral award. Contracting will give you more direction on whether you have to sign it or not.

Step 4.

Step 4 is to communicate with contracting about the next steps. There's going to be some sort of start of work meeting or pre-con, depending on what type of work it is. This is where a notice to proceed (NTP) is going to be issued. When you win an award, you don't just start doing the work. There still has to be a meeting of the minds between you and contracting and the COR, and whoever else is going to be engaged, to make sure everyone is on the same page with the same plan.

For example, what is the exact day you're going to start? What is that process going to look like? Does something have to be finished before you can get started? All good questions, and more, need to be discussed.

Sometimes the contract is awarded, but they're still waiting for funding for it. Another reason why we don't just start working is if the money isn't there for contracting yet to pay you. So, you want to make sure there aren't any funding issues. You don't necessarily have to ask them about it, but be aware of it if it's something that they mention.

This is the time to gather base access information, specifically for your sub. If you have not already, there's information in your contract that you have to submit and send over regarding who's going to need to get on base, etc. This is going to be the time to start getting that flow of communication to contracting, as well as any government training like iWatch (this would be included in your contract) for those accessing the base should be performed at this time.

The start of work meeting itself could be on the phone or it could be in person. If all goes well in the meeting, you will be issued a notice to proceed with a start date. From here, you can have your teaming partner begin mobilizing, ordering, or whatever they have to do to get ready for the job. It's at this time that it's also good to review the contract deliverable requirements so you can meet your milestones on time once the contract officially gets started.

Step 5.

Step 5 is to prepare for invoicing. The most commonly used invoicing system is called Wide Area Workflow (WAWF). There are other systems, and it's typically going to take around 60 days to get through setup and have your first invoice payment issued. After that, you will be able to submit regular invoices each month and have payments regularly every 30 days.

You're going to have to learn the invoicing system for your contract like WAWF. It's going to take a little bit of time initially. Sometimes your invoices can get pushed back. There can be issues with you putting amounts in the wrong area because you don't know what you're doing yet.

You do get instructions for setup from contracting, but they can be hard to follow. You will also be given a point of contact from the agency's payable department. I recommend as you're going through this initial setup that you communicate with the contracting officer and whoever that POC is in payables on the government side. This helps to make sure you're doing everything you can to speed up the process.

If you do have a different invoicing cycle than recurring monthly, then you're more than likely looking at a project-based contract, a construction contract, or some sort of product drop-shipping contract. For project-based contracts, you will be paid when the contract is completed and contracting has signed off on completion. For construction, there will be milestones that you meet, and when you meet them a percentage of funds will be released. With products, payment is released once delivery is made and quality checked.

In all of these instances, it's incredibly important to be communicating with whoever is going to be signing off on quality and completion because they control how quickly you will get paid. If you match one of these contract types, be clear with contracting at the start of the contract how and when you are going to be paid, and don't be afraid to ask questions. Contracting wants you to get paid as quickly as possible so that there is no break or disruption in service.

CONTRACT MANAGEMENT

It's a lot of work to win a contract. And when you first win, it's very exciting and you want to celebrate. You should celebrate, pat yourself on the back, and allow yourself to feel good. With that in mind, the real work is just beginning. One game has finished, and another has just begun. Learning this game and understanding what's required of you now as the responsible prime contractor is key to your long-term success. Let's get set up for long-term success and dive into the game of contract management.

Communication

Success in the contract management game is going to be reliant on strong communication throughout the entirety of contract performance. We've touched on the communication needed for a start-of-work meeting, but it doesn't end there. To best illustrate this picture, let's have a quick refresh of the parties involved.

Contracting Officer: This is the only person who is able to interpret the contract and obligate funds, which also includes making changes to the contract. They are technically "the boss." Direction for your team should only come from the contracting officer.

Contracting Officer Representative (COR): This person is able to enforce the contract only. They cannot interpret the contract or make any changes. This is the person who will be the one who is onsite during your work performance, and so their feedback is the one that reflects the quality of your service on the contract.

Prime Contractor: This is you. The prime contractor holds the contract directly with the government and is ultimately responsible for meeting all requirements. The prime contractor is also the one to whom payment is released directly. The prime takes direction directly from the contracting officer. The prime takes direction from the COR solely based on what is written in the contract.

Subcontractor: This is your teaming partner. As a team, you are going to accomplish the requirements of the contract. The subcontractor shall only take direction from you (the prime contractor) because their contract is a commercial one (B2B) with you. They do not have a direct contract with the government.

COR

What I've been personally involved with, and have seen happen quite often, is the COR thinks they have more power than they really do. Needless to say, it can be a tough situation to navigate because, in instances like this, it can feel like you're trying to serve two masters—the Contracting Officer and the COR. Since the COR does not have the power to interpret or make changes, all they can do is enforce the contract as is.

Problems can arise when the COR wants something done differently than what's written in the contract. Since they are the one after all who is onsite, unlike the contracting officer, they can feel very comfortable throwing their opinion around. This puts you in a tough spot because you know your quality marks will be coming from this person. But you also know this person *technically* cannot tell you or your team what to do. It has to come down from contracting.

So how do you best navigate this and protect yourself at the same time?

Yes, you want to hear the COR out. If it's just enforcing the contract, then that's not even what we're talking about here. If a situation arises, however, and something different from what's written is being mentioned or proposed, your spider sense needs to be going off.

Hear them out and listen to what they have to say. You may even agree with what they're suggesting. Let them know what they say makes sense, and you will send an email to the contracting officer and CC them (the COR) on the email as well to update the contracting officer on what you plan to do.

What you're really doing is signaling for contracting to dive into the contract to see if what's being proposed is permitted. If it is, then great. If not, contracting will be the one to shoot it down and it won't be your fault, so you're not sacrificing your relationship with the COR. Now, if this change is something you are not in favor of, you will want to present evidence from the contract as to why the change is detrimental, would require a contract modification, or changes in funding.

The main point here is to avoid going along with things just because the COR says so. I've seen it so many times where the

COR tells the prime to do something outside of the contract. Then, when the Prime does that and the contracting officer finds out, the COR just points to the Prime and plays dumb. Or worse yet, while doing the out-of-scope work, something costly happens and now the situation needs to be explained from the beginning. And it's going to be pinned on you, the prime contractor, to eat the damages.

Protect yourself by communicating with the Contracting Officer anytime you have a COR who is trying to throw their weight around too much. It may seem scary because you're trying to keep the peace, but if you don't, it can end up so much worse for you.

Request for Equitable Adjustment (REA)

If something does arise in the contract that requires you to perform out of the scope of work, you are entitled to a request for equitable adjustment (REA)[15]. If there is something unforeseen that occurs that you can prove there is no way you could have known, then you are entitled to compensation on the contract to make you whole again, so you can perform the full service. Similarly, if contracting misled, provided incorrect information, straight up missed something, or forgot to include something in the statement of work, you are entitled to be additionally compensated for those costs.

If you are in this situation, email the contracting officer requesting an equitable adjustment. They will invite you to make your case and you will explain the situation and the cost. If accepted, they will ask you to provide the updated costs for reimbursement for the past period that you have been operating at a loss and the remaining period of performance for the duty.

An REA won't save you if you cannot make a strong case. If you just missed something (or your sub), then you will be forced to eat the difference and still have to provide the full service per your contract. It's all the more important that you and your partner review the requirements of the work fully when quoting, attend any site visit, read all the questions asked by other companies, and submit your own questions to contracting to avoid missing something important.

CDRLs

We've mentioned this previously, but once your contract is underway, you want to be on top of any and all deliverables that are required in your contract. These will directly be linked to how your overall performance on the contract will be rated. Deliverables that you may need to complete by certain dates can include reporting, an updated quality control plan, updated licenses and credentials, ongoing meetings, quality inspections, and the timely meeting of project completion milestones.

Deliverables will go to the COR and the Contracting Officer. These are important, but it's certainly okay to ask questions or communicate about anything that's being required or asked of you. I often say it seems very black-and-white communicating with contracting before you win the award. They either want to talk to you or they don't.

Once you win and have a contract with them, then you are now in a long-term relationship with them, and it goes from black and white to grey. Their success is tied to your success, so they often become much more helpful and communicative once you have an award with them.

CPARs Rating

You are given an interim CPARS rating and a final rating. Think of this as your report card. CPARS stands for Contractor Performance Assessment Reporting System. When you have a CPARS rating to show, contracting officers will be able to access and review your performance on previous contracts as part of a past performance evaluation. If you have a contract that was terminated, for example, it's going to look very bad, and contracting is going to be very apprehensive to work with you again.

On the other hand, if you have glowing CPARS ratings, it can just as much be very beneficial to you. You nurture and cultivate strong CPARS ratings through strong communication and performance on the contract. For example, I had won a contract to staff 4 people but none of my candidates showed up for their first day of work.

Can you say nightmare scenario? Contracting was furious, and I thought they were going to terminate us on the spot. We were able to talk them down and start sending them backup resumes immediately. By the end of the 2.5 years on that contract, I don't think they remembered it anymore, and we put extra effort into the performance of that contract, and we received glowing CPARS ratings in the end.

This is a real example of what can happen, but it doesn't mean all is lost. This example is really bad, but smaller annoyances happen all the time. Contracting knows nothing is perfect and things do happen.

For them to terminate a contract is going to make an even bigger problem for them. So, when something happens, you are usually aligned with fixing the problem and moving on. It's up to you to be the leader though and give contracting confidence that there is a way out of this problem.

CONTRACT EARNINGS MULTIPLIERS

As an add-on from our earlier discussion of your Agency earning's potential, there are additional ways to "juice the lemon", that can enable you to thrive using competitive margins so that you ultimately profit more on your contracts. You only need to get good at one or two of these to start using them consistently to make a large scalable difference as you grow your GovCon Agency. Remember, over time, an inch becomes a mile. I would encourage you to read through these and make note of the earning multipliers that resonate with you so that once you start winning contracts, you can begin to practice applying them.

Win More

Although obvious, I still need to get this one out of the way. It may sound flippant to tell you to "win more contracts" when you haven't won any yet, but you will find that over time you are in more control of winning than you think. Once you have developed a base of winning one contract per quarter, for example, you will know the amount of work it takes to achieve that, and then you can make the decision to throttle up or down depending on what you feel like doing or what your strategy is for the particular time of year.

This is very much a number's game, with quality being more important than quantity. The more you bid, the more you win. And usually, the less you bid, the less you win. You don't start out winning, you start out learning. If you stick with it, you will eventually reach a momentum point where you start winning consistently 5-10 contracts per year, and maybe more. You will learn that you can set your activity level to match how much work you can handle.

What you can handle will expand over time. Continuing to build the library of your own company proposal content to pull from will make proposal writing more efficient. Learning from proposal debriefs with contracting officers will make you wiser. As you practice finding Deals and contacting subs, it is virtually impossible for you to not skill up. For these reasons, you will be able to handle more overtime.

Once you get really good, you eventually reach a point of diminishing returns. At this time, you can consider bringing a partner, an intern, or a spouse to teach them the same process. This will be a geometric leap in what you will be able to handle, and will allow you to dramatically increase the number of contracts you are able to win if you expand properly.

Organic Growth

Organic growth in government contracting is the opportunity for more work that comes from the initial contracts that you win. In other words, some may call it the Lifetime Value (LV) of a government customer. Some even go as far as pricing their first contracts on the lower side because they know they are good at cultivating organic growth with a customer. You shouldn't start out using this LV principle, but knowing that it exists underscores the real potential that organic growth can offer to your Agency.

A few quick tips for you to include in your first contract wins to optimize for organic growth include:

Tip #1 Intentionally build positive relationships with the Contracting Officer and Contracting Officer Representative.

Tip #2 Educate yourself and research the other opportunities that exist on site.

Tip #3 Educate the government points of contact on the other areas of work your company is capable of performing (preferably after you learn about the other opportunities they have). You can do this subtly in conversations or you can schedule a capability briefing with them to more formally share your competencies.

Tip #4 Don't be afraid to ask contracting if they have anything on SAM.gov that they are currently quoting, or if they have anything on their desk that they need quotes on from small businesses. I would much rather respond to a solicitation that contracting has asked me to respond to over one where contracting doesn't even know I exist. I prefer this tip to be used during the busy season (July-Sept) where there are more opportunities going around for everyone before the fiscal year budget ends on September 30.

Tip #5 Build other relationships with anyone else from the government that is associated with your contract. They are likely working on other contracts simultaneously and have knowledge of other work. These titles can include engineers, program managers, and other folks in contracting.

Higher Margins

Depending on the type of contract and how it's being evaluated, some contracts allow for higher margins than others. When I say allow, I don't mean formal permission is given. I mean you can be competitive at higher margins.

We've touched on this, but you can achieve higher margins by responding to Best Value evaluated contracts as opposed to Lowest Price Technically Acceptable (LPTA) contracts. I recommend that you do both, and have a healthy mix of both in your pipeline as they both have their own advantages. As we discussed in the reading phase for solicitations, you can develop the skill of quickly identifying which evaluation method is being used in order to respond appropriately and strategically.

Another strategy to achieve higher margins is the Alternative Proposal Strategy. Not a lot of contracts know about this, and you can use this approach unless the government explicitly states, "No Alternate Proposals", which they sometimes do. So, unless prohibited, you can submit an alternate proposal.

An alternate proposal is a secondary proposal submitted separately from the first proposal where you give them everything they've asked for in the way they've asked for it.

In the alternate proposal, you are providing a different approach to completing the work that will result in higher value to the government. In reality, it's going to have to be a really good alternate to be considered outside of what they've requested. But you never know. If, for example, you have a subcontracting teaming partner that has a new or innovative method that they can accomplish the work, in some instances, even at a cost savings for the government, you can still include a slightly higher margin than typical to accompany the alternate approach. Again, you submit both proposals because we know there is a fair chance the alternate would not be competitive, so you still have your original proposal response for consideration.

Larger Contracts

Another somewhat obvious statement, but something that really comes into your realm of possibilities over time is targeting larger contracts. You may find that small contracts can be tedious, but so are large ones. So, many GovCon Agencies decide over time, and through experience, that they are going to focus their efforts on larger contracts so that their input of work results in more output. There's not a huge difference in growing from individual \$100,000 contracts to \$500,000-\$1M contracts.

In the government's eyes, these are still considered to be very small. They are above-simplified acquisition procedures, so you will want to make sure your legal middleman approach is consistent with the dollar value, but other than that, you're solving a bigger problem, you're making more money, and the contracts are not that much more difficult to manage at this increased size.

If it's difficult to imagine yourself winning and performing on a \$1,000,000 contract, I understand. It's a big number, and psychologically it takes time to catch up because most of us don't have many references in our lives to compare that number to. I promise, it does not take long to come to terms with performing a million-dollar contract, especially if you have previous wins under your belt. You will want to push your perceived dollar size limits in no time!

Self-Performance

This is the Legal Middleman Method, but that doesn't mean that you can't learn to self-perform work, too. Think about it. You will have managed and successfully completed projects through working with your teaming partner, and if you pay attention, you should have a pretty good idea of what it takes to do this yourself. I don't mean to personally do it yourself, but to hire or assemble a team within your company to do the work instead of an outside company.

Doing this can grow your company by leaps and bounds. It certainly comes with more responsibility and management, but you also can be a lot more profitable. Just imagine if you didn't have to go to subcontractors to get quotes, and you could make a Deal or No Deal decision within your agency because you have team members who can already estimate and perform the work. It certainly changes things, and it can also make you that much more competitive in your proposal responses so then you will win more contracts, too.

The total thought isn't to totally change lanes to self-performance once you have several wins under your belt. But there's absolutely nothing wrong with having a blended approach where some contracts you Legal Middleman, and eventually, maybe there's a particular industry that you learn to self-perform on, too. The industry should be whatever industry you're winning the most in and has proven that it will make sense to double down on and start self-performing.

Contract Modifications

There are a few different scenarios where you can get additional funding through contract modifications onto the existing contract that you're performing under that would increase your total profitability, as well as the lifetime value of your customer.

The first is to examine if there is parallel or simultaneous work that needs to be done alongside your existing contract. For example, if you have a construction project and there is an environmental component required, that could be filled by a different contractor as a separate scope of work. Or if you are providing logistics services in the form of a delivery truck driver, but then they have a warehousing person who receives the goods. Existing or upcoming needs that parallel your contract are items to be aware of because, through the cultivation of strong relationships, it's possible to have your contract modified to expand the scope of work and add services so that you can perform these parallel functions through your company.

Second, this is not a true modification. But it is a reminder that when you have base-year contracts with option years, the option years are not guaranteed. It's up to you to provide confidence to the government that it will be in their best interest to execute options years rather than competing with a new requirement.

It is the lowest hanging fruit that exists for you to have your contracts extended to the maximum periods they can be.

Next, figure out if there is additional scope that's related to the direct work you are doing that can be added to the contract. We see this a lot in staffing positions where it's not a parallel service that needs to be added, it's just literally more of the same that you're already providing.

Does your customer have another location where the same thing is being done through recompete contracts each year? Is that something they can add to your contract since you now have a positive track record of performing well on your scope of work at their main location?

Last, we've mentioned it before, but Requests for Equitable Adjustment (REA) exists to make you whole when your company is asked to perform a service that is out of scope and you are not being compensated for. Once an REA is submitted, reviewed, and approved, these additional funds will be released as a result of an invoice to reimburse additional costs incurred on the contract. This is not something to be used as a tactic or strategy like the others. REAs only exist to protect your company and make it whole again if it has suffered an unfair loss.

Profitability through Subs

As previously mentioned, negotiating with subs is a great way to increase contract profitability as long as you don't push them past the point of being interested in doing a good job for you. Many subs will build in a cushion to their numbers, so not negotiating just means you are leaving money on the table. For subs expecting to be negotiated down, not negotiating can signal that you are new to managing another company, and they could see that there is a gap in your armor to try to take advantage when other opportunities may arise. You want to have healthy boundaries in a prime-sub relationship, and a big part of that comes from acting the part.

A second way to gain additional profitability on a contract is by incentivizing your subs to finish early. It may not apply to every scope of work, but it makes sense on some contracts to incentivize the subcontractor to finish sooner than the projected completion date (project-based contracts).

Finishing the project early can dramatically reduce direct and indirect costs. By incentivizing your teaming partner with a small cash incentive to finish early, your investment can go over great with the relationships you've established with the government POCs on the contract who will be in disbelief when the project finishes earlier than expected.

Do a Good Job

Sometimes, not everyone is able to do a good job on a contract. Sometimes, the contract was doomed from the start. Other times, your teaming partner does not perform the way they are supposed to. There are also times when the Contracting Officer and the COR do not agree, and you're stuck in the middle. Or, the contract has kicked off but something is preventing you from starting, like insufficient funding.

All these factors (and more) can make it difficult to do a good job from start to finish on a contract. With that being said, setting the intention to strive to always do a good job can go a long way. Contracting officers have been burnt many times by contractors who just don't seem to care about the contract at all.

They don't communicate at all. They do a terrible job. This is why contracting goes to great lengths to vet contractors to not only get the most value but to also ensure the contractor who's chosen will hopefully do a good job by following the guidelines of the contract.

You can never do a good job without communicating. So, it's paramount to remain in constant communication. Situations do happen, like in my example earlier where my 4 staffed positions didn't show up for their first day of work. Doing a good job also means professionally working through situations as they arise.

It seems so lackluster to have "Doing a Good Job" be the bar that you set for yourself, but it's really what contracting needs, and it's what so many contractors are unable to do. What you've learned in this book should more than equip you with what you need in order to do a good job.

FINAL THOUGHTS

Now, it's time to tie everything together and share my final thoughts with you. We have covered so much in this book, and if you've made it this far, then you've done great! Use this book as a resource to come back to again and again. Make notes, highlights, and whatever you need to do to use the information contained herein and apply it to your GovCon Agency.

Overview

If you are a big-picture person and high-level thinker like me, you like to have everything boiled down to its essence, so you can understand how it all comes together. So, here is an overview of everything we've covered and exactly what you need to do to move forward with short and defined steps:

- You need to find a bid on SAM.gov.
- You need to read through it and decide if it's something you want to invest in bidding on. If it's a no, you move on. If it's a Deal, next, you find multiple subs who can quote it.
- Call the subs and go through the intro call process that I laid out. If you can't find any subs, you're dead in the water, so move on to another bid. If you have at least 2 subs to

bid, share details of the job so they can attend a site visit or begin quoting the work. Help them to give you accurate pricing and proposal support if needed.

- While you're doing this, begin putting together your proposal response to the government, including any government forms. To do this, you will want to use the 5-phase bid process that we provide in the Bids training module (read, outline, price, proposal, submit/debrief).
- You will also want to email contracting to ask if there is an incumbent or if there is a new need. If there is an incumbent, you can ask for the contract award number so you can look up the previous value to try to inform your pricing.
- When putting your proposal response together, do this strategically according to whether or not it is a best value or LPTA bid. Be sure to submit as many RFI questions as needed before the Q&A deadline, including questions from your subs.
- Once you have the quote from the sub, and you've put everything together in your proposal, review your proposal or have someone else review it, and then submit your offer to contracting.
- Once an award is made (to whomever), ask for a debrief.
- Contracting can be slow to get back to you, so feel free to follow up with them every couple of weeks (depending).
- If you win, complete your teaming agreement with your selected teaming partner, and sign and return the award to contracting.
- Communicate with contracting to receive a notice to proceed from the government and commence work.

- Ensure to meet contract deliverable deadlines.
- Invoice the government and get paid (pay the sub).
- Manage the contract to ensure positive CPAR ratings.
- Continue playing the numbers game by bidding to win new contracts, and leverage earnings multipliers to grow more contracts from the contracts you've already won.

Upcoming Challenges

Just like with anything in life, there are possible challenges that you will come up against. So, instead of you discovering those on your own and going through the emotional drain and distraction that comes with that, I want to share with you what could come up so you can be mentally prepared.

At first, you could feel intimidation, overwhelm, paralysis analysis, and imposter syndrome. These are things that I hear very frequently. If this is you, it's normal. Just follow the process that we have laid out. Getting quotes from subs is going to take practice, and communicating with subs is going to be new to you. You're probably going to suck at it, and that's okay, because if you know you're supposed to suck at it, then you won't get so down on yourself if you're not good yet.

Maybe you don't suck at it, maybe you start out being okay or even average, and that's awesome. Many of you are extremely resourceful or you have other business experience. So, you may not have to encounter all of these challenges, and that's great if you don't have to.

For many, there are no issues communicating with subs, right? So, I don't want to plant the seed saying it has to be that way. But if you do get a little bit of confusion about what to say or unsure how to respond to feedback, just work through it. It's going to be fine, and you will get better.

Next is communicating with contracting officers. This can be slow. It can be frustrating at times when you've responded to a bid and you haven't heard back. There's not a whole lot we can do aside from continuing to follow up. The most important thing is to know that it could happen so that when it does happen, you don't get all geeked out about it. We keep following, but we also move on to the next bid to focus our mental energies there.

Assembling bid proposals is also not something that comes overnight. This is going to improve over time. Most of you are not professional writers. You're going to be building your library of content for your company the more you respond to bids. And then you have your sub's content to help put together the response as well. You can also submit questions to contracting to help with any place you're stuck with formatting or writing for the bid proposal.

With all of this being said, I want you feeling good. I want you feeling optimistic. I want you feeling encouraged. But I also want you to be realistic. I want you to have this realistic radar of expectations and upcoming potential challenges.

Do Not

I don't want you to try this for a couple of months and quit. Okay? That for me is the biggest insult. I've seen so many do that, and I've also seen so many go on and be successful, and it's become very clear to me that it's your choice. Do not give up on yourself when it gets hard. When it gets hard, many quit, and only the deserving who persevere are rewarded.

And there's no reason why you are any different from others that have been successful. You're not different. The only reason that would make you different is if you quit, or you start believing things that are untrue, like you can't do this or it's just too hard. These are just steps in a process that obtain certain results. You just have to do it.

For every action, there is a reaction, right? Do the thing, and then something will happen. Especially if you do it consistently over time. So, to help you with this, I invite you to not think in terms of days and weeks. Think in terms of months and years. You're building a business after all, and everybody easily agrees it should take two or three years to really get a business off the ground.

But when it comes to government contracting, for some reason, everybody wants to do it in two or three months. No, give yourself 12 to 18 months. If you set your sights here, you'll have things happening well under that time period.

So next, do not get distracted by other things that you hear on YouTube, TikTok, Instagram, or even LinkedIn. I know there are other coaches out there, and I know there's a lot of stuff being said specifically in our industry about "How to win your first government contract."

Following multiple strategies at the same time often results in no strategy. It is the fastest way to go nowhere. If you are here, trust me to be your coach, put your blinders on for everything else, and commit. It is one of the common ingredients that I see amongst those who are successful long-term.

So, if you want to be successful, then you must be very focused. You're jumping in the deep end of the pool and doing it, and you're trusting in your resourcefulness to push through fear and resistance as it comes. Do that, and you will be successful. I strongly believe you can because I've seen it happen so many times.

EXPECTATIONS

I have been in federal contracting for 10 years now. For the last five of those years, I have been coaching and consulting directly with small businesses, specifically small businesses that are brand new to federal contracting. I've seen many of those businesses go on to be successful, and I've also seen even more give up, burn out, or throw in the towel because they say it's too hard. One of the biggest correlators that I see with this is the small businesses' expectations coming in.

I find that the better aligned and the better-managed expectations can be right from the start, the better chance they have at persevering through potential setbacks that can throw them off track. Having the right expectations going in and understanding how you should play this game will strengthen you and keep you focused on working the Legal Middleman Method as we describe in this book.

Let's look at Seasonality and The Numbers Game to best set our expectations going forward.

Seasonality

Seasonality is the fluctuations in business cycles over time. Seasonality is something that is very real in federal contracting, and it is something that we do not have control over. If we can manage our expectations, this won't catch us off guard, instead, we can take advantage of it. As is famously said, "When winter comes, we can either freeze or we can learn how to ski." So, we want to play to the seasonality. We don't want to be a victim of it.

Q1- When I say seasonality, what I specifically mean is that there are going to be busier times and slower times throughout the year. The federal contracting landscape and the fiscal year are broken down into four quarters. And it does not mirror a calendar year.

October 1st is the new year in federal contracting, so the first quarter spans October 1st to December 30th. During this time, contracting will have come off of a very busy season. During this quarter, contracting is taking vacations. They are not behind their desk. They are not very responsive, and they have just finished the busy season. They are at a point of waiting for the funding for the new year to come in, meaning they don't have a whole lot of money to spend on new contracts for the new year just yet.

During this time, you can see more sources sought being posted, more market research, and maybe some new year forecasts, but not a lot of awards necessarily being made, aside from existing contracts coming to an end and starting anew, and also contracts for snowplowing and road salt can be procured during this time.

Yes, overall spending does go down during this quarter, but then the spending that does happen is not zero. It's not like there are no contracts. It's just less. It's just a dip in the curve. So, we're managing our expectations and we're kind of sharpening our saw during this period.

Q2- In the second quarter, Q2, things start to warm up a little bit. It begins right after the calendar new year, January 1st, at a time when people are getting back to their desks. It's that new year high people kind of come in with, and it feels the same with contracting. Things start to warm up a little bit. Maybe a little bit of funding has come through, but probably not a whole lot at this time.

But more specifically, contracting is looking to just kind of start getting more projects pushed out to set up for this new year. You'll see a bit more awards being made, and more importantly, you'll see a lot more opportunities put out on SAM to start looking at. Again, it could be upstream, it could be only sources sought or it could be pre-solicitations; not necessarily all solicitations yet.

Q3- But then when you get to Q3, a lot of those opportunities are ready to be solicited and awarded. Again, there are opportunities and contracts to be awarded throughout the entire 12 months, but we are aligning ourselves with the expectations of the season. Now, with the warming up of the season, and more awards being made, we should be working a lot harder—later nights and some weekends to start reaping the harvest.

Q4- Once July hits, it's Q4. The busy season is in full swing. July through September is when most awards are being made. Previously, a lot of opportunities were being put out on the street so that they could be awarded in these subsequent months. Now is that time. We really want to be best positioned to take advantage of this time of year so that we can essentially bid on and win as many opportunities as we can handle for our service agencies.

The Number's Game

Finally, let's shift to your personal timeline for federal contracting. Being able to set reasonable expectations for the numbers you should try to hit gives you something to gauge your progress against. For those that I work with, I like to see a first bid submitted in your first 30 days. It's highly possible. I even see multiple bids submitted from some in their first 30 days, so you can do it. I believe in you! If you have life events that happen or that are stopping you at the moment, that is understandable. But without those distractions, you should be able to accomplish the 30-day milestone.

By month 3, you should have submitted at least several additional bids. I do see some awards come in during this stage because you're starting to put some numbers on the board, and that's what can happen once you start consistently responding.

If you've responded to 4 or 5 bids, then you're in the realm of an award becoming possible. And for some, it's just kind of getting lucky. So, you could have just gotten lucky, but that's what happens when you put yourself out there. Good things can happen!

By month 6, you are certainly feeling more confident. You're starting to be more strategic in the bids that you're responding to. And because you've now responded to 5-10 bids at this point, your responses are getting better. You are stacking proposal content that you've written in your proposals, and now you're able to reuse that. Hopefully, you've received at least one, if not a couple of debriefs from contracting by now, and it's certainly possible that you've won one or a couple of contracts at this stage.

During months 6-12, you should absolutely have won something by now (possibly multiple contracts.) But you have to be playing the numbers game while improving. By the end of the year, you should aim to respond to 10-20 contracts.

Write this down. "10 to 20, you're in the money." That's your ultimate goal. When you reach this range, the odds are very much in your favor for winning—especially if you're using all the processes that I've given you in this book and are constantly improving your responses and skills.

For some, they will have nothing to show after this time period because they were not consistent with it. The Numbers Game is not just bidding. It's bidding with improvement. If you keep doing the same things wrong 10 or 15 times and you're not winning, well that's just a waste of your time. This is what's realistic for you. I've seen it time and time again, and there's no reason why you should be any different. Do the work, learn, be consistent, and do it for long enough to have it pay off for you.

ACKNOWLEDGMENTS

This book is symbolic of so many important moments in my life, and those who were behind the scenes supporting me during them. Without them, this would not have been possible.

Thank you, Mom and Dad, for always being my rock and safety net. Always knowing where home is has been a privilege that not everyone gets, and that has allowed me to take risks and strive to be all that I can be in life. Without you, I wouldn't have been able to reach as far as I have and continue to do.

Thank you, Lala, my partner. You were the person who was there right beside me when this crazy journey began. I was crying, you were there for me, and I made the decision to leave my job having no idea that starting this business and touching this many lives was waiting for me. We've had so many long nights, stressed conversations, and heated moments. We've also had so many amazing moments and celebrations. Through it all, you have been my biggest cheerleader and the one who knows the depth of everything that I have struggled through. Thank you for supporting me and loving me unconditionally.

Thank you to my best friend, BJ. I've always looked up to you as an older brother even though we're the same age. You've never turned me away, and you're one of the *very* few people who I always know will show up for me whenever I need you. We are not related by blood, but our bond is even stronger.

I thank the younger version of myself for following my heart and never giving up on ME, when there were so many moments when I wanted to quit.

I thank you, God. I know you are always with me and your hand has been guiding me for longer than I can remember. My biggest hope is that one day I can even slightly come close to making a little difference (for good) in this crazy world and that I would have made you proud.

ABOUT THE AUTHOR

Derek James has been passionate about government contracting for more than a decade. He continues to work with small businesses to implement the Legal Middleman Method so they can build a GovCon Agency that empowers them to live their lives in the direction of their dreams.

Through his ever-growing government contracting YouTube channel, transformational courses and programs, and overall expanding presence in the space, Derek's teachings are responsible for tens of millions of dollars of government contracts being awarded to the small businesses that follow him across the country.

Derek learned only in his adult life that he has neurodivergent brain functions that affect how he processes information. School and college were extremely frustrating times for him, but now he prides himself on being a different type of learner. He brings this energy and compassion for learning along with a knack for creating simple examples to cultivate deeper levels of focus and understanding for those small business owners who feel overwhelmed and anxious trying to learn government contracting.

Growing up, Derek found himself on a 10-acre property in a small farm town in Southeast, MI. He still loves the wide-open spaces. Today, he lives in Gulf Shores, Alabama, where his number one priority is spending time with his family.

As a drummer, he loves going to rock concerts. He is incredibly passionate about animals. Derek loves playing his favorite childhood computer game, Age of Empires II. He's performed for a few open mic nights at comedy clubs. And he tries to walk each day in stride with God.

In 2023, Derek and Lala visited Ireland to meet with Lorna Byrne, a well-known author most known for her book, *Angels in My Hair,* and they shared a life-changing experience. Derek commented, "Lorna is building a spiritual sanctuary that will be around for hundreds of years, and it's going to attract so many people once the word gets out. Anyone who is deeply struggling with something in life, who is trying to have a deeper relationship with their spirit, or who just wants a trip of a lifetime should visit Lorna and her daughter Pearl at the Sanctuary in Thomastown, Ireland." Visit lornabyrne.com and tell them Derek sent you.

APPENDIX

1. Pass-through: https://www.acquisition.gov/far/52.215-23
2. Limitations on Subcontracting (LOS): https://www.acquisition.gov/far/52.219-14
3. Simplified Acquisition Procedures (SAP): https://www.acquisition.gov/far/part-13
4. FAR Part 13.5: https://www.acquisition.gov/far/subpart-13.5
5. Utilizing Subcontractor Past Performance: https://www.acquisition.gov/far/15.305
6. Industry Report: https://www.legalmiddleman.com/bookbonus
7. Umbrella Strategy: https://www.legalmiddleman.com/bookbonus
8. Sub Site Visit Checklist: https://www.legalmiddleman.com/bookbonus
9. Wage Determinations: https://sam.gov/content/wage-determinations
10. USA Spending: https://www.usaspending.gov/search
11. FPDS.gov: https://www.fpds.gov/

12. GSA eLibrary: https://www.gsaelibrary.gsa.gov/
13. Smallpdf: https://smallpdf.com/
14. Debrief Questions: https://www.legalmiddleman.com/bookbonus
15. RequestforEquitableAdjustment:https://www.acquisition.gov/dfars/252.243-7002-requests-equitable-adjustment.

The Legal Middleman Method

Visit legalmiddleman.com to start
Legal Middlemanning today.

Printed in the USA
CPSIA information can be obtained
at www.ICGtesting.com
CBHW050357111223
2393CB00007B/3

9 798989 068265